Sense-Abilities

Sense-Abilities

Fun Ways to Explore the Senses

Activities for Children 4 to 8

Michelle O'Brien-Palmer

CHICAGO
REVIEW
PRESS

Library of Congress Cataloging-in-Publication Data

O'Brien-Palmer, Michelle.
   Sense-Abilities : fun ways to explore the senses : activities for children 4 to 8 / Michelle O'Brien-Palmer.
   p.   cm.
   Includes index.
   Summary: Presents activities that delve into the characteristics of our five senses,
allowing readers to predict outcomes, gather materials, make scientific observations, and respond to their findings.
   ISBN 1-55652-327-0 (alk. paper)
   1. Senses and sensation—Juvenile literature.   [1. Senses and sensation—Experiments.
2. Experiments.]   I. Title.
QP434.O347   1998
612.8—dc21   98-22983
                                                           CIP
                                                            AC

Design and Ilustrations: ©1998 by Fran Lee

©1998 by Michelle O'Brien-Palmer
All rights reserved
Published by Chicago Review Press, Incorporated
814 North Franklin Street
Chicago, Illinois 60610

ISBN 1-55652-327-0

Printed in the United States of America
5 4

Sense-Abilities is dedicated to
Professor William M. Muse,
scientist, lifelong learner, and educator.
Professor Muse shared his love of science
and the scientific process of discovery
with such passion that his students
became forever . . . scientists.

Contents

The Process of Discovery

A scientist discovers by checking things out.
The process of discovery is what it's all about.
We use our senses and exercise our minds
As we think, explore, observe, and tell you what we find.

Sung to "The Itsy Bitsy Spider"

Introduction for Parents and Teachers

Sense-Abilities is about you and me, and the way we make sense of our world through our five senses. Each sensory activity is designed to be fun and simple and to promote learning by engaging children in a process of self-discovery. Even very small children become eager scientists as they predict outcomes, gather materials, make scientific observations, and respond to their findings. Learning about the wonders of each sense through these hands-on activities provides instant information and introduces children to the scientific process of discovery that they will use in their scientific inquiries for the rest of their lives.

The format used in each *Sense-Abilities* activity is purposeful. It reflects the progression used in any scientific exploration. The basic concepts have been preserved as children are transitioned into the process of discovery using language that is familiar to them. Each activity begins with the phrase "Did you know?," which corresponds to *research* and new information. "You will need" introduces children to the *materials* needed to conduct their experiments. With the phrase "What do you think?," every activity allows the child to make an outcome prediction, or *hypothesis*. "Now you are ready to" explains the *procedure* one would follow in testing the hypothesis. The "Brain exercise" gives children an opportunity to draw *conclusions* from their scientific observations.

Each chapter begins with a poem that can be sung to a familiar tune. The chapter contents are described in "All About . . . ." The sense being explored is discussed on the "Abilities" page. Lively, fact-filled nonfiction books and picture books are referenced in "Read All About It!" They are a wonderful complement to the activities. The language used to describe our sensations ultimately forms the foundation for great literature. Journal sheets are provided to help children record and reflect as they connect language, artwork, and learning. Make as many copies as you need.

All activities have been field-tested successfully in homes and classrooms. Most require simple materials that can easily be adjusted to accommodate your children. In these cases exact quantities of materials have not been specified. Estimated yields are given for the baking and lemonade-making activities.

Initially, all of the activities will require adult supervision. After completing the activities together, many parents and teachers choose to set up learning centers using some of the activity materials on the sense being explored. Children can then test the sense on their own during the week. This is a great way to extend and expand learning.

Sense-Abilities is an adventure in understanding the wonders of our senses, nature, and ourselves. As children delve into the characteristics of each sense, they will also temporarily experience what it would be like to live without it. They will explore braille and the world of those without vision as well as sign language and the world of those with hearing losses.

Join together with your children as you re-explore the sensational abilities of your senses!

—*Michelle*

All About Sight

My Eyes

I have two eyes so I can see
flowers, trees, birds and bees.
I have two eyes so I can see.
I can see you and me.

My two eyes see left and right,
black and white, 'n colors bright.
My two eyes see left and right.
I see in day and night.

Sung to "Mary Had a Little Lamb"

4

In All About Sight you will find

Read All About It!

Author	Title	Publisher
Aliki	*My Five Senses*	HarperCollins, 1989
Allan Fowler	*Rookie Read-About Science Series: Seeing Things*	Childrens Press, 1991
Mem Fox	*Hattie and the Fox*	Aladdin, 1992
Heweston/Jacobs	*Eye Magic: Fantastic Optical Illusions*	Guild Books, 1994
Tara Hoban	*Look, Look, Look*	Greenwillow Books, 1998
Rachel Isadora	*I See*	Greenwillow Books, 1985
Reese Lindberg	*Midnight Farm*	Dial Books, 1987
Bill Martin	*Brown Bear, Brown Bear, What Do You See?*	Henry Holt, 1992
Bruce McMillan	*Sense Suspense: A Guessing Game for the Five Senses*	Scholastic, 1994
Jane Moncure	*The Look Book*	Childrens Press, 1982
Maria Rius	*The Five Senses Series: Sight*	Barron's, 1985
Cynthia Rylant	*The Relatives Came*	Bradbury Press, 1985
William Steig	*Brave Irene*	Farrar, Straus & Giroux, 1986
Rosemary Wells	*Night Sounds, Morning Colors*	Dial Books, 1994
April Wilson	*Look! The Ultimate Spot-the-Difference-Book*	Dial Books, 1990

Sight-Abilities

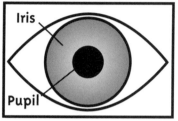

Iris

Pupil

Why is your sense of sight important?

✪ Your eyes are shaped round like a ball. That is why eyes are sometimes called eyeballs.

✪ We can see between 150 and 200 different colors.

✪ The black dot in the middle of your eye is called a pupil. The colored part of your eye that surrounds the pupil is called an iris. You may have the same-colored iris as your friend or a different-colored iris.

✪ The iris is a ring of muscles that make the pupil larger or smaller, depending upon the light you are in. In a dark room your pupils will get larger so more light can come into your eyes. In a light room your pupils will get smaller.

✪ Tears wash dust and unhealthy particles out of your eyes automatically. They protect your eyes and keep them moist and healthy.

✪ Your eyes work together to determine how far away things are from you. This is called depth perception.

✪ The location of your eyes on your head affects what you see, since each eye sees objects from a different perspective.

✪ A small part of each eye is not sensitive to light. This is called your blind spot. The blind spot is small and you don't notice it when you are using both eyes.

✪ Your eyes can see in front of you and to your sides too. Side vision is called peripheral vision.

✪ Your eyes help you to identify many important things. They tell you about the shape of an object. Your eyes can tell what things mean very quickly. Certain shapes are very important to know, like the symbol for poison that warns us about our safety.

✪ Your eyes give you information about an object even if you can't see all of it. Just seeing the outline of a familiar object is usually enough information for you to identify that shape.

✪ Eyes are very sensitive to light. Protect your eyes in bright sunlight by wearing sunglasses and not ever looking directly into the sun.

My Sense of Sight Journal

Today I learned

Right Light? Bright Pupils

Did you know?
The black dot in your eye is called a pupil. It changes size depending upon the amount of light in a room.

You will need
Room that is dimly lit when the lights are off
Partner

What do you think?
If the lights are turned off, my partner's pupils (will) or (won't) get larger.

Now you are ready to
1. Find a partner.
2. Keeping the lights on, look closely at each other's pupils. Are they big or small?
3. Turn the lights off.
4. When your eyes have adjusted to the new light, look at each other's eyes again. What happened? Did they change?
5. Turn the lights back on and check each other's pupils again. Why do you think pupils change size?

Brain exercise
When the lights were turned off, my partner's pupils got . . .

Activity Goal	Sensory Note	Key to Success	Hint
To experience how the eye changes to let in light or keep out light.	The iris is a ring of muscles. It makes the pupil dilate or contract to let in the right amount of light for optimal vision.	Use the eye diagram on page 7 to introduce the iris and the pupil.	If the room is too dark the children won't be able to see the pupil change. Very dark eyes are harder to see pupil changes in than lighter eyes.

Did you know?

Your eyes work together to tell you how close or far away things are to you. This is called depth perception.

You will need

Large-holed plastic needle
Thin cord or ribbon
Eye patch

What do you think?

If I have my left eye shut, I (will) or (won't) be able to thread a needle.

Now you are ready to

1. Using both eyes, thread the plastic needle with a ribbon.
2. Cover your left eye with the eye patch, or just shut it.
3. Try to thread the needle using only one eye. How does it work?
4. Ask a friend to try this activity.

Brain exercise

When I tried to thread the needle with only one eye, it was . . .

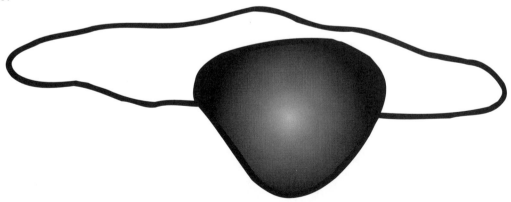

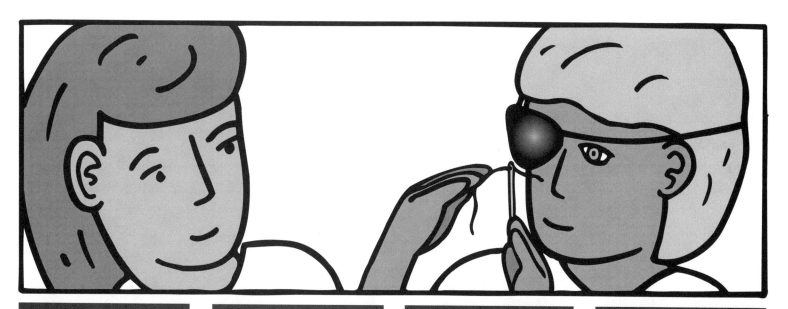

Activity Goal

To introduce the concept of depth perception.

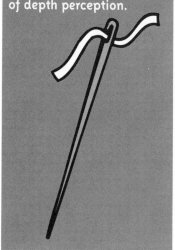

Sensory Note

Depth perception gives the world a 3-D quality. It is just one more gift our eyes give us.

Key to Success

The cord or ribbon you select must easily fit into the needle's eye. Children must be shown how to thread a needle before they start this activity. To take the activity a step further, ask the children to switch the eye patch to the other eye and ask if it affects the needle-threading experience. If it is much different for a child, you might consider a visit to the eye doctor.

Hint

To promote an even greater understanding of depth perception, ask children to wear an eye patch for a certain length of time and report the differences between seeing with one eye and two.

3 Moving Vision? Two Right Eyes

Did you know?
The location of your eyes on your head affects what you see.

You will need
Just you

What do you think?
If I look at my finger with my right eye, it (will) or (won't) look the same as when I look at my finger with my left eye.

Now you are ready to
1. Put your pointer finger out in front of you.
2. Look at your finger with your right eye only first and then with your left eye only.
3. What happens? Why do you think this happens?

Brain exercise
When I looked at my finger using different eyes, . . .

Activity Goal	Sensory Note	Key to Success	Hint
To experience the different visual perspectives of each eye.	Each eye sees objects from a different perspective. This is why your finger looks like it has moved when you look at it from first one eye and then the other.	Children need to be able to close one eye and then open the other.	If your children have trouble closing one eye, have them focus on a clock or other object as they place a hand over one eye and then over the other.

4 No Light, No Sight! Blind Spots

Did you know?
There is a small blind spot in each of your eyes.

You will need
PicStick pattern page 14, copied onto card stock
Crayons or markers
Scissors
Tongue depressor or popsicle stick
Glue

What do you think?
If I bring the PicStick close to my eye, I (will) or (won't) be able to see both pictures the whole time.

Now you are ready to
1. Color your PicStick and cut it out.
2. Glue the PicStick square to the top section of the tongue depressor.
3. Cover your left eye and slowly bring the PicStick closer to your eye. At some point you won't be able to see the crayon. This means that you have found your blind spot.
4. Share your PicStick with your friends.

Brain exercise
When I looked at the PicStick, my eye . . .

Activity Goal	Sensory Note	Key to Success	Hint
To identify a visual blind spot.	Part of the retina is not sensitive to light. Where the optic nerve enters the brain there are no rods or cones to transmit light or color.	The PicStick must be moved slowly and the left eye kept covered.	If children are worried about their blind spots affecting their vision, let them know that when both eyes work together we don't even notice the blind spot.

PicStick

Sense-Abilities, ©1998. Published by Chicago Review Press, Inc., 800-888-4741.

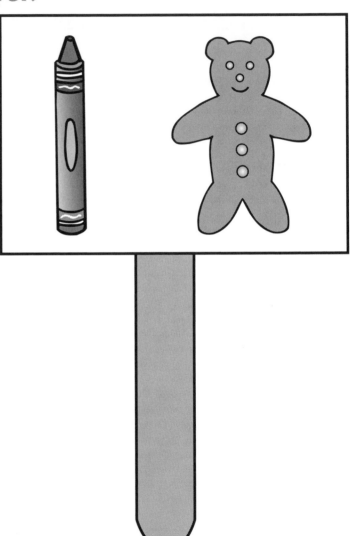

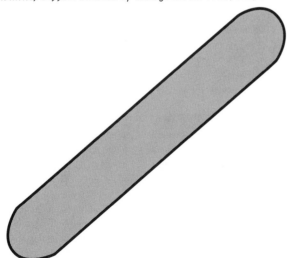

5 Side Sight? Peripheral Vision

Did you know?

Your eyes can see in front of you and to your sides, too.

You will need

Children's sunglasses (party glasses come 4 to a package)

Dark painting marker

PicStick from No Light, No Sight! Blind Spots

What do you think?

If I wear sunglasses with blacked-out lenses, I (will) or (won't) be able to see.

Now you are ready to

1. Use the dark painting marker to blacken the lenses of the sunglasses. Let them dry.
2. Put on the glasses.
3. Hold the PicStick in front of you. Can you see it?
4. Now move the PicStick to the side of your face. Can you see it?

Brain exercise

When I tried to see things on the side, my eyes . . .

Activity Goal	Sensory Note	Key to Success	Hint
To introduce the concept of peripheral vision.	Peripheral vision is an important factor in driving and riding a bike. It gives us vital information about our environment.	Make sure the glasses fit and children don't walk around or play while wearing the glasses, as they limit vision.	Keep glasses at a learning center with the PicStick.

6 Special Shapes—Short Cuts

Did you know?
Your eyes help you to identify different shapes. Certain shapes give you important information in a very short time.

You will need
Special Shapes sheet page 17, copied onto card stock and laminated if possible

What do you think?
If I see a sign with the shape of a person, I (will) or (won't) know which shape means the right bathroom for me.

Now you are ready to
1. Look at box 1. Do you know what this shape means?
2. Repeat step 1 with each box on the sheet.

Brain exercise
When I saw the flag shape, my eyes told me . . .

Activity Goal	Sensory Note	Key to Success	Hint
To identify shapes that give us important information about our world.	We use shapes as symbols to represent consolidated information. Our eyes collect data and our brains interpret the significance and meaning of each shape.	Before you start, discuss different symbols like Mr. Yuk and the No Smoking sign.	This activity can teach children more about important symbols in their lives.

Special Shapes

7 What Is That? Eye Detectives

Did you know?

Your eyes give you information about an object even if you can't see the whole thing.

You will need

See and Guess sheet page 19, copied onto card stock and laminated if possible

Partner

What do you think?

If I don't see the whole picture, I (will) or (won't) be able to tell what is in the box.

ANSWERS: 1. Baseball player 2. Plane 3. Mom at a computer 4. Cowboy on a horse

Now you are ready to

1. Look at each picture box on the sheet. Ask your partner to guess what is in each box.

2. Tell your partner what you think is in each box.

3. If you disagree, read the answers or ask an adult to help you.

Brain exercise

When I saw the picture in each box, my eyes . . .

Activity Goal	Sensory Note	Key to Success	Hint
To experience how our eyes fill in the details when we can't see the whole picture.	Just seeing the outline of a familiar shape can give us enough information to identify that shape.	Ask a group of children to identify one of the pictures. Then let them try in pairs or individually on their own.	This activity is fun for people of all ages. You might want to try making your own pictures out of cut-up magazine artwork.

See and Guess

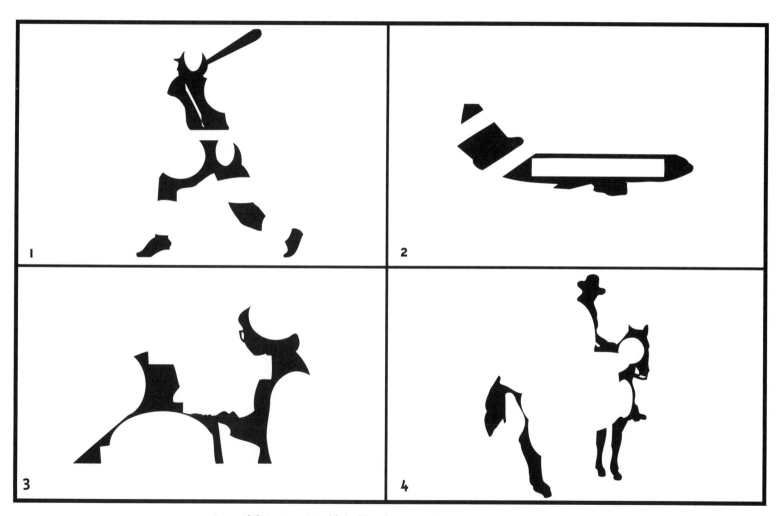

8 Seeing Is Believing—Different Sight?

Did you know?
Two people can look at the same picture and see different things.

You will need
Picture cards 1 and 2, pages 21 and 22, copied onto card stock and laminated if possible

Partners

What do you think?
If I look at the picture cards, I (will) or (won't) always see the same thing as my partners.

Now you are ready to
1. Look at picture card 1. What do you see?
2. Ask your partners what they see. Do you all see the same thing?
3. Follow steps 1 and 2 with picture card 2.

Brain exercise
When I looked at the picture cards, I saw . . .

Activity Goal	Sensory Note	Key to Success	Hint
To experience viewing a picture from many different perspectives.	Sight is affected by the life experiences of the viewer. We interpret what we see through our understanding of what things are and how things work. We perceive our environment through our past and present connection to it.	Make sure you give each child a chance to say what he/she sees. No answer is wrong.	This makes a great group activity. Children enjoy hearing each other's ideas.

Picture Card 2

9 See and Say Color Match

Did you know?
Most people can see many different colors.

You will need
12 crayons (2 of each color)

Partner

What do you think?
If I see a crayon, I (will) or (won't) be able to match it with the same-colored crayon.

Now you are ready to
1. Take the wrapping off all 12 crayons. Mix them up.
2. Match the crayons to each other.
3. Ask your partner to match the crayons.

Brain exercise
When I saw the different crayons, my eyes . . .

Activity Goal	Sensory Note	Key to Success	Hint
To identify and match 6 different color pairs.	We can distinguish between 150 and 200 different colors.	Younger children need crayons that are very different from each other in color.	To challenge older children, find colors that are more and more similar until they can't distinguish between them.

Did you know?
Your brain stores and creates pictures of the world so that you can see without even opening your eyes.

You will need
Song from a favorite movie

Classical piece unfamiliar to the children

Tape recorder or CD player

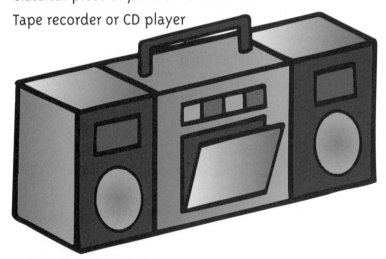

Now you are ready to
1. With your eyes closed, listen to a song from one of your favorite movies. What do you see in your mind?
2. Listen to a piece of classical music you have never heard before. What pictures do you see in your mind? What do your friends see in their minds?
3. Talk about the different pictures each person sees.

What do you think?
If I shut my eyes when I hear a song, I (will) or (won't) be able to see a picture in my mind.

Brain exercise
When I listened to the classical music, . . .

Activity Goal

To experience mental images stimulated by sound rather than open eyes.

Sensory Note

The mind will bring up familiar pictures from a movie that everyone has seen. These pictures come from memories of a shared experience. Our minds will create unique pictures based upon the tone and tune of the music when we listen to an unfamiliar piece. These pictures come from our imaginations.

Key to Success

For the movie selection, try to use music from a movie everyone has seen. For the classical selection, choose an unfamiliar piece of music.

Hint

If the children have trouble focusing on the music, let them wear blindfolds to remove visual distractions.

11   Watch That Color—Make a Color Wheel

For each Color Wheel, you will need

ι 3-inch-wide circle cut from card stock

ι earring post

ι earring clutch

ι balsa-wood strip 1/4 inch wide and 4 inches long
(this is the handle)

Bright-colored markers

Now you are ready to

1. Use the markers to color the round circle with bright designs.
2. With an adult's supervision, push the earring post through the center of the circle and into the top middle section of the balsa-wood handle.
3. Place the earring clutch on the post back to keep it from hurting anyone.
4. Spin the circle and see how your design changes.

Brain exercise

When I spun the circle, I saw . . .

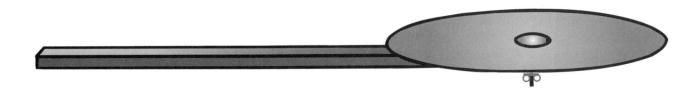

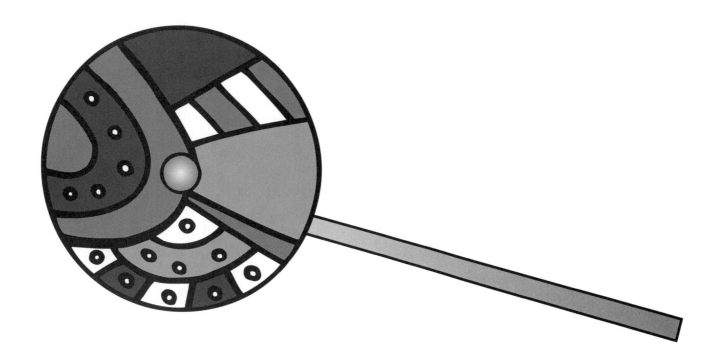

Activity Goal	**Sensory Note**	**Key to Success**	**Hint**
To show how eyes respond to colors moving at different speeds.	Our eyes tend to blend the colors together as they speed up.	The Color Wheels work best when the earring post goes through the center of both the circle and the balsa-wood handle.	This activity requires adult supervision. Although the posts are not sharp, they could possibly harm a child if enough force was used. The clutch helps protect children after they make the wheel.

What do you think?

If I go to an aquarium, I (will) or (won't) find fish with eyes very different from mine.

You will need

To visit an aquarium

Now you are ready to

1. Visit an aquarium.
2. As you look at the different fish, notice their eyes. Do most fish have eyes like yours?
3. Look for the *seastars* (starfish). Do you see eyes on the seastars? Look at the ends of their arms to find their light receptors.
4. Find a fish called *sole*. Did you know that they start out with one eye on each side of their heads, but as adults both eyes are on the same side? One eye rotates to join the other as the fish matures.
5. See if you can find the *four-eyed fish*. It can see on top of the water and under the water too.
6. Look for a *flashlight* fish. It has very interesting eyes that shine light through the water.
7. What other interesting fish did you find?

Brain exercise

When I went to the aquarium, I saw . . .

Activity Goal

To discover the differences of eye placement in fish and other marine life.

Sensory Note

Marine animals' eyes are positioned to help them catch their food and stay safe.

Key to Success

Being located close to an aquarium makes this activity more convenient.

Hint

Children really enjoy focusing on the eyes of the marine life as they explore the aquarium. This field trip gives children the opportunity to read or be read to, draw pictures, and record their learning.

13 What If? No Sight!

Did you know?
People who can't see use their other senses to help them make sense of the world.

You will need
Blindfold

Egg timer

What do you think?
If I can't see, I (will) or (won't) use my other senses to help me.

Now you are ready to
1. Set the timer for 10 minutes.
2. Put on the blindfold. Walk or move around with an adult or another person to help you so that you don't hurt yourself while you can't see.
3. What was it like to be without sight? How did you feel when others were moving about and you didn't know what they were doing? Was it hard to tell where you were? What other senses did you use to help you? What dangers might there be if you couldn't see?

Brain exercise
When I couldn't see, I was . . .

Activity Goal	Sensory Note	Key to Success	Hint
To temporarily experience what life might be like without the sense of sight.	In the dark our vision is limited to black and white. We depend on our senses of hearing and touch to guide us.	Talk about the senses we would use if we were blind.	Adult supervision and guidance is needed so the child doesn't get hurt while blindfolded.

14 Reading Without Eyes

Did you know?
People who can't see use their sense of touch to read.

You will need
12 braille circles, page 33, copied onto card stock

2 braille letter boards, page 34, copied onto card stock

Scissors

Rubber cement

Braille alphabet sheet, page 35, copied onto card stock and laminated if possible

Sandpaper (fine 150)

Marker

What do you think?
If I can't see, I (will) or (won't) use my sense of touch to help me read a letter in braille.

Now you are ready to
1. Place the sandpaper behind the card-stock braille circle sheet. Cut the circles out.
2. Match your pieces. Glue the back of the sandpaper cutouts to the card-stock cutouts.
3. Using the braille alphabet sheet on page 35 as your guide, form an alphabet letter by placing the sandpaper circle cutouts onto the appropriate squares of the braille letter boards.
4. Try making another alphabet letter using the other braille board.
5. To make the letters permanent, glue the circles to each braille letter board in the patterns shown on the braille alphabet sheet. Write each letter on the back of its board.
6. Close your eyes and feel the pattern. Can you tell which letter you are feeling?

Brain exercise
My fingers read the letter. . .

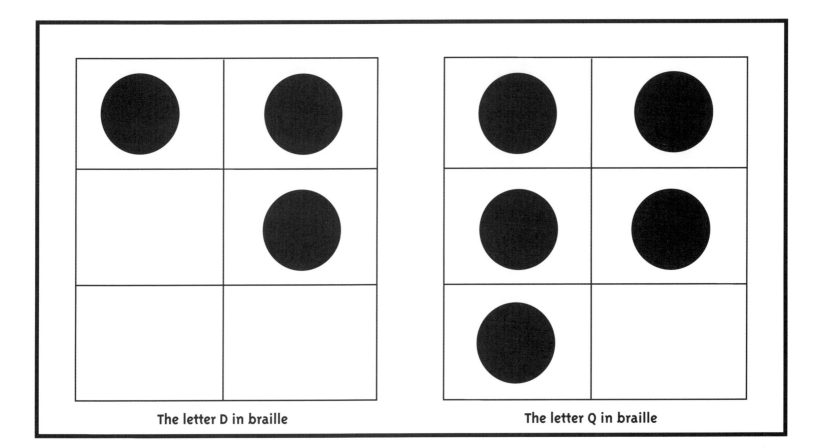

The letter D in braille

The letter Q in braille

Activity Goal

To use the sense of touch to communicate a letter.

Sensory Note

Certain types of sandpaper are too rough for the skin of small children. Fine 150 works well.

Key to Success

Make as many braille letter boards as possible. It's fun for children to pair up and test their skills at identifying letters using a blindfold.

Hint

To challenge children, ask them to write their names using the braille letter boards.

Braille Circles

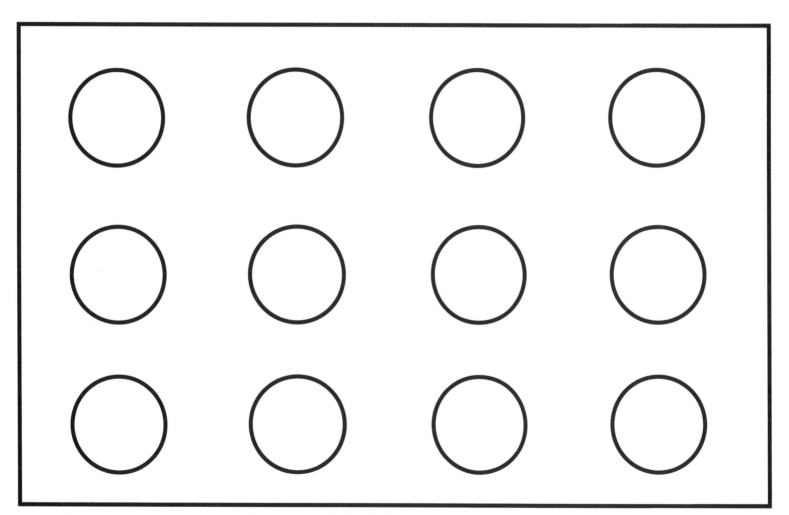

Braille Letter Board

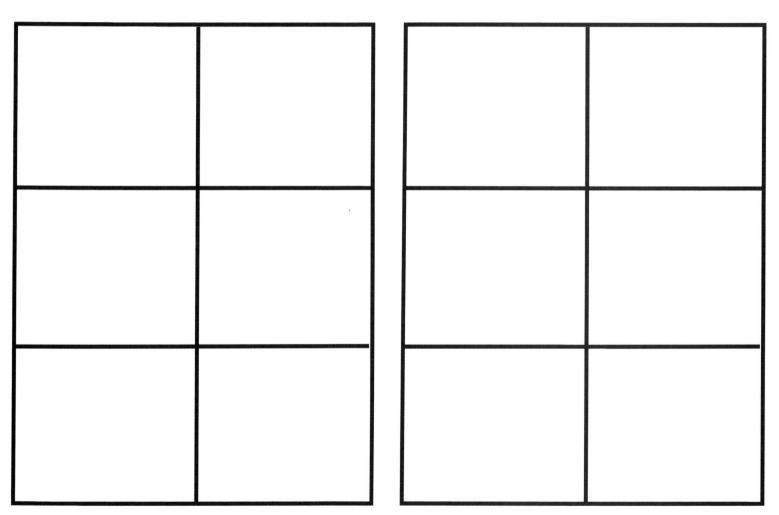

Braille Alphabet

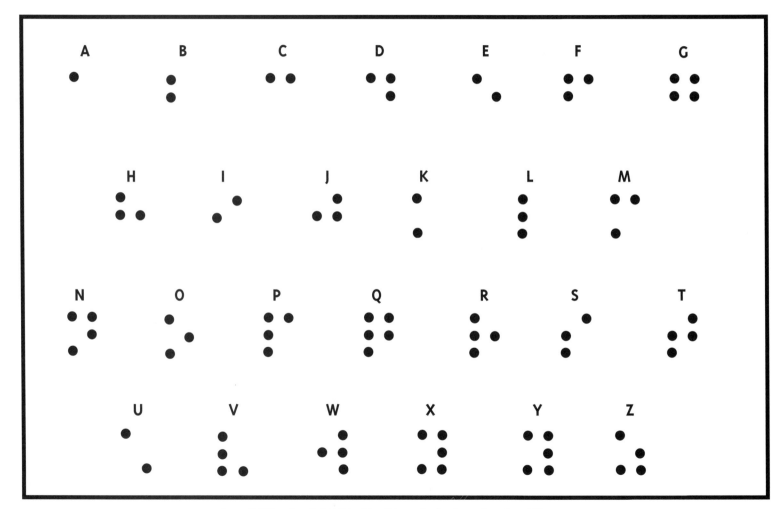

15 Walk About and See

Did you know?
You use your sense of sight more than any other sense.

You will need
To be outdoors

Child-size earplugs

What do you think?
If I go outside, I (will) or (won't) be able to identify many things in nature by my eyes.

Now you are ready to
1. Walk outside and look around. What do you see?
2. Sit in one spot. Put the earplugs on. Do the sights change? Do you recognize the things that you saw earlier?
3. Take off the earplugs. Draw pictures or write about the things you saw.
4. Think about words that describe what you see.

Brain exercise
When I walked outside, I saw . . .

Activity Goal	Sensory Note	Key to Success	Hint
To explore the sights in the environment.	We see objects in our environment most clearly when we are not distracted by our other senses.	It's nice to go somewhere new. The sights are more vivid and inspiring.	If you stay in a familiar environment, try looking at it from a mouse's, cat's, or dog's perspective to spice up the activity.

All About Touch

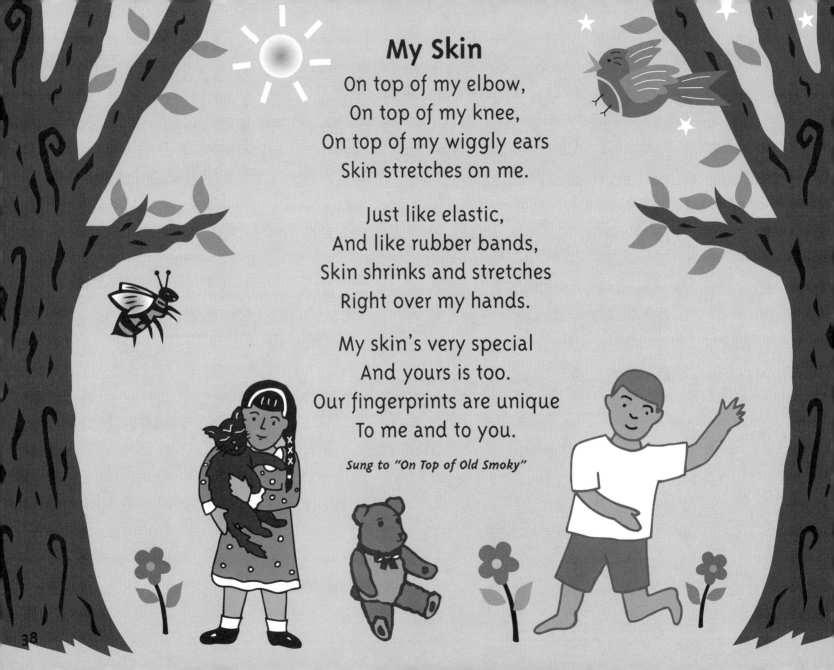

My Skin

On top of my elbow,
On top of my knee,
On top of my wiggly ears
Skin stretches on me.

Just like elastic,
And like rubber bands,
Skin shrinks and stretches
Right over my hands.

My skin's very special
And yours is too.
Our fingerprints are unique
To me and to you.

Sung to "On Top of Old Smoky"

In All About Touch you will find

Touch

Read All About It!

Author	Title	Publisher
Aliki	*My Five Senses*	HarperCollins, 1989
Eric Carle	*The Very Busy Spider*	Philomel Books, 1995
Monica Byles	*Experiment with Senses*	Lerner Publications, 1994
Henrik Drescher	*Pat the Beastie*	Hyperion, 1997
Allan Fowler	*Rookie Read-Aloud Science Series: Touching Things*	Childrens Press, 1991
Tara Hoban	*Is it Rough? Is it Smooth? Is it Shiny?*	Greenwillow Books, 1984
Rachel Isadora	*I Touch*	Greenwillow Books, 1991
Bruce McMillan	*Sense Suspense: A Guessing Game for the Five Senses*	Scholastic, 1994
Jane Moncure	*The Touch Book*	Childrens Press, 1982
Maria Rius	*The Five Senses Series: Touch*	Barron's, 1985
Cynthia Rylant	*The Relatives Came*	Bradbury Press, 1985
Cynthia Rylant	*When I Was Young in the Mountains*	Dutton, 1982
William Steig	*Brave Irene*	Farrar, Straus & Giroux, 1986
Rosemary Wells	*Night Sounds, Morning Colors*	Dial Books, 1994

Touch-Abilities

Why is your sense of touch important?

✪ Your skin is the largest organ in your body. It includes your fingernails, hair, toenails, tongue, and the inside of your mouth, nose, and ear canals. It covers your whole body.

✪ Your amazing skin shrinks and stretches as you bend and stretch. This makes it easy for you to move in different directions.

✪ Your fingers are more sensitive to touch than any other part of your body. They give you important information about the world around you.

✪ You can identify an object just by its texture. You can tell the difference between a slippery apple and the uneven peel of an orange or a warm, fuzzy tennis ball and a hard, cold golf ball without using any other sense but touch.

✪ You know when something is soft, rough, patterned, or fuzzy. The sense of touch lets you feel if something is hard like a rock or squishy like a bean bag.

✪ Your fingers can also identify an object by its shape. You can tell the difference between a banana and an apple by their shapes.

✪ Your fingers are very sensitive to temperature. You know when something is hot, cold, or warm just by touching it.

✪ The sense of touch lets you determine if something is wet or dry.

✪ There is no one else in the world who has the same fingerprints as you do. Your fingerprints are unique.

✪ The sense of touch protects you from harm by warning you when you touch something that is too hot. You feel pain and then quickly move your hand away. It lets you know if the bath water is too hot to be safe.

✪ Our skin is sensitive and needs to be protected from the harmful rays of the sun. This is why it is so important to wear sunscreen.

My Sense of Touch Journal

Today I learned

Stretch and Shrink Magic Tattoo

Did you know?
Skin shrinks and stretches as you bend and stretch.

You will need
Caterpillar or other insect tattoo stickers (removable)

Wet sponge

Rubbing alcohol

What do you think?
If I put a caterpillar tattoo sticker on the inside of my arm and stretch, it will . . .

If I put a caterpillar tattoo sticker on the inside of my arm and bend, it will . . .

Now you are ready to
1. Straighten your arm and place a tattoo sticker on the inside of your elbow.
2. Follow the directions on the tattoo package. (This usually includes a wet sponge. Most tattoos come off with rubbing alcohol.)
3. Once the tattoo is dry, stretch your arm out in front of you. What do you see? Is the caterpillar long or short?
4. Bend your arm in a little. What happened to that caterpillar? Did it get longer or shorter?

Brain exercise
When my arm is stretched, the skin . . .

When my arm is bent, the skin . . .

Activity Goal

To experience skin shrinking and stretching.

Sensory Note

The largest organ of the body is skin.

Key to Success

Use a large enough tattoo to see the size difference as the child stretches and bends his/her arm. If you are working with a large number of children, it might be better to put the tattoo on your arm to do this activity. You can then show it to the children.

Hint

Make sure to get a tattoo that is easily removable.

2 Fingers or Toes? Touch Test I

Did you know?
Your toes are more ticklish than your fingers.

You will need
Tennis ball

What do you think?
If I touch a tennis ball with my fingers, it will feel (the same) or (different than) when I touch a tennis ball with my toes.

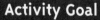

Now you are ready to
1. Take off one of your shoes.
2. Touch the tennis ball with your fingers.
3. Touch the tennis ball with your toes. Does the tennis ball feel the same as when you touched it with your fingers?

Brain exercise
My fingers are . . .

Activity Goal	Sensory Note	Key to Success	Hint
To note the difference in sensitivity between the toes and the fingers.	Our fingers are more sensitive to touch than our toes because there are many more receptors in our fingers.	Ask children to pet the ball with their pointer finger and then pet the ball with their big toe. The sensation gets confusing when they use different parts of the hand and foot.	Be prepared for very interesting socks and feet. You might want to tie in the senses of smell and sight in this activity.

3 Finger Detectives! Touch Test II

Did you know?
You can identify an object just by its texture.

You will need
Blindfold

Partners

Sturdy paper bag

Assorted objects with similar shapes but different textures, like the following, placed in the paper bag:

Small apple

Kiwi fruit

Small peach

Lemon

Tennis ball

What do you think?
If I am blindfolded, I (will) or (won't) be able to tell the difference between the items in the bag.

Now you are ready to
1. Put on the blindfold.
2. Have one of your partners help you reach into the bag. Pull out an item.
3. Touch the item. What do you think it is? Describe it for your friends.
4. Take off the blindfold and see if you are right.
5. Take turns guessing the items in the bag with your partners by repeating steps 1 through 4

Brain exercise
When I touched the items in the bag, my fingers . . .

Activity Goal

To identify and describe the textures (slippery, rough, fuzzy) of different items.

Sensory Note

Our fingers give us multiple clues to help us identify an object.

Key to Success

Younger children may need to use their sense of smell to help them identify the items successfully. To challenge older children, try using items that are very similar to each other.

Hint

Use fresh, not-quite-ripe fruit. The fruit is very tempting to young children. Remind them that we are scientists and the only time we eat our experiments is when we are learning about the sense of taste.

4 Hot or Cold? Touch Test III

Did you know?
Your fingers are very sensitive to temperature.

You will need
3 coffee mugs, 1 containing cold water, 1 containing very warm water (close to hot), and 1 containing warm water

Large plastic container, like a plastic dishpan

What do you think?
If I touch cold water, I (will) or (won't) be able to identify it as cold.

Now you are ready to
1. Set the filled coffee mugs inside the plastic container.
2. Put your left pointer finger in the cold water. Does it feel cold?
3. Place your right pointer finger in the hot water. Does it feel hot?
4. Count to 10 two times.
5. Take your fingers out of the mugs and put them both in the warm water.
6. What happened? Was your brain confused?

Brain exercise
When I put both of my pointer fingers into the warm water, my brain . . .

Activity Goal	Sensory Note	Key to Success	Hint
To identify cold, warm, and hot water and to experience the confusion of too much information at one time.	When our brains get too much sensory information at once, we get confused.	Make sure that the water isn't too hot for the children.	This can be messy. It helps to set the mugs in a plastic container.

5 Grab Box! Touch Test IV

Did you know?
You can identify objects just by their shape.

You will need
Partner

An assortment of very differently shaped items placed inside an empty upright tissue box:

Child's small plastic paintbrush

Wrapped Tootsie Pop

Fun-shaped arts and crafts sponge

Tree leaf

Very small ball

Small rock from your yard

Small eraser

Feather

What do you think?
My partner (will) or (won't) be able to identify the objects in the box by their shape.

Now you are ready to
1. Ask your partner to select an item in the box.
2. Ask him/her to tell you what it is before he/she pulls it out.
3. Repeat steps 1 and 2 as you take turns with the other objects in the Grab Box.

Brain exercise
When my partner touched the things in the box, his/her fingers . . .

Activity Goal

To identify different objects by their shapes.

Sensory Note

Our sense of touch gives us much more information about objects than just texture. We can easily identify objects by their shapes.

Key to Success

Items need to be familiar to the children and of very different shapes.

Hint

For an activity extension, try using two boxes with the same items inside and have children match them.

6 Fingers That Hear My Vibrations!

Did you know?
You can feel vibrations as well as hear them.

You will need
Just you

What do you think?
If I sing a song, I (will) or (won't) be able to feel the sound on the front of my neck.

Now you are ready to
1. Feel the front of your neck with your hand.
2. Say "Hello!" Did you feel the sound? Try coughing, laughing, and growling.
3. Sing your favorite song and feel the vibrations through your neck.
4. Can you feel how the vibrations change places? Why do you think you can feel your voice?

Brain exercise
I can feel my voice on my neck because . . .

Activity Goal
To experience different sound vibrations through touch.

Sensory Note
When we speak, our vocal cords vibrate to create each sound. This vibration can be felt through the front of our necks.

Key to Success
Hands should be placed gently over the voice box (larynx).

Hint
Introduce the concept of vibrations prior to this activity.

7 Tricky Towels—Wet or Dry?

Did you know?
Your fingers have the ability to tell you if something is wet or dry.

You will need
Blindfold

Partner

Sink

Dry towel

Slightly damp towel

Damp towel

Wet towel

Dry

What do you think?
I (will) or (won't) be able to identify a wet towel.

Now you are ready to
1. Put on the blindfold.
2. Have a partner place the 4 towels in front of you.
3. Feel each towel. Set aside the dry towel.
4. Take the blindfold off and see if you were right.

Brain exercise
When I touched the towels, my fingers . . .

Activity Goal	Sensory Note	Key to Success	Hint
To distinguish between wet, dry, and damp.	Our fingers give us information about temperature, wetness, shape, pressure, and texture.	Younger children may need you to start with wet and dry and then move up to different levels of wet. Older children like to touch all of the towels first and then rate them as to the moistness.	Have the towels prepared before you start. This activity can be messy unless a sink is used.

8 What's That Feeling? Feeling Frame

Did you know?
You can tell when something is soft, rough, patterned, or fuzzy.

You will need
2 3-inch squares of light-colored burlap

2 3-inch squares of white satiny material

2 3-inch squares of white velvety material

2 3-inch squares of white monk's cloth

2 3-inch squares of quilt batting

Fabric glue

2 8 ½-x-11-inch sheets of colored card stock (red works well)

Mitten- or hand-shaped die-cutting pattern (or picture mat with 5 openings)

Blindfold

Partner

What do you think?
If my partner touches a piece of fabric, he/she (will) or (won't) be able to describe what it feels like.

Now you are ready to
1. Use a die-cutting pattern to cut a design in the corners and center of 1 sheet of card stock. Save the cutouts for later.
2. Glue 1 square of each type of fabric to the back of each opening in the card stock. Save the remaining fabric squares for the Touch and Match Fabric Grab Bag activity, page 55.
3. Spread glue along the back sides and in the center of the decorated card stock. Attach the remaining sheet of card stock to the glued back. Turn over to make sure the frame is straight.
4. Pull the batting out a bit so it puffs out.
5. Ask your partner to put on the blindfold and help him/her to touch each piece of fabric.
6. Ask your partner to tell you what it feels like.

Brain exercise
When my partner touched the fabric, . . .

Activity Goal

To identify different textures.

Sensory Note

One of the most pleasurable characteristics of the sense of touch is that we can identify many wonderful textures.

Key to Success

If you change the fabrics, make sure that they are different enough from each other to help younger children feel successful.

Hint

If you don't have your own remnants, buy material from a fabric store in 1/8-yard portions and share the extra material with other teachers or parents. This will make 5 complete sets. Check your local craft store for a die-cutting machine, or recycle a picture mat with 5 openings.

9 Touch and Match Fabric Grab Bag

Did you know?
Your fingers can match one texture with another.

You will need
- 1 3-inch square of light-colored burlap
- 1 3-inch square of white satiny material
- 1 3-inch square of white velvety material
- 1 3-inch square of white monk's cloth
- 1 3-inch square of quilt batting

(Use the extra squares from the Feeling Frame, page 54.)

Paper lunch bag (decorate it with the mitten or hand cutouts from the Feeling Frame activity, if you like)

What do you think?
I (will) or (won't) be able to match the fabrics in the lunch bag.

Now you are ready to
1. Look at the Feeling Frame. Touch one of the fabrics.
2. Without looking inside, reach into the lunch bag and feel for a matching fabric.
3. Pull the matching fabric out of the bag and see if you were right.
4. Repeat steps 1 through 3 until all of the fabrics have been matched.

Brain exercise
When I tried to match the fabrics, my fingers told me . . .

Activity Goal	Sensory Note	Key to Success	Hint
To match fabrics by touch only.	Our fingers can easily identify items by their textures.	If children are having trouble completing this task, ask them to feel a piece of material first and then identify the fabric on the Feeling Frame.	Use the leftover cutout hands or mittens from the Fabric Frame to decorate items for other activities.

10 Touch Testing—One End or Two?

Did you know?
Certain places on your arm are more sensitive to touch than others.

You will need
Blindfold

Partner

2 small plastic-handled children's paintbrushes with narrow ends

What do you think?
I (will) or (won't) be able to tell if the narrow ends of 2 paintbrushes are touching me.

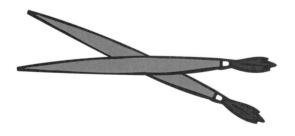

Now you are ready to
1. Ask your partner to put on the blindfold.
2. Carefully take 1 paintbrush and touch the narrow end to the skin of your partner's inner arm. Did he/she feel 1 end or 2?
3. Carefully take 2 paintbrushes and touch the narrow ends to the skin of your partner's inner arm. Did he/she feel 1 end or 2?
4. Try steps 2 and 3 on different parts of your part ner's arm and then on his/her neck just below the hairline.
5. Ask your partner to try testing you with the paint brush ends, changing the order of the touch tests.
6. Try testing your own skin with the brush portion of the paintbrush. Where is your arm the most sensi tive? What does it feel like on your lips? On your fingertips?

Brain exercise
When the narrow end of the paintbrush touched my arm and neck, my skin told me . . .

Activity Goal

To test the sensitivity of your arms to touch.

Sensory Note

Some places on our arms are more sensitive than others. The more sensitive areas can tell the difference between two paintbrush ends or one.

Key to Success

Use paintbrushes with narrow ends that are about the same size.

Hint

Give the children lots of time to explore on their own.

‖ Perfect Prints Thumbprint Art

Did you know?
No one has the same fingerprints as you do.

You will need
Play clothes or apron

Crayons or markers

Paper towels

Washable colored ink pad

Soap and water

Plain white paper

Partner

What do you think?
If I put my thumb on the ink pad and then put it on the paper, my thumbprint (will) or (won't) be the same as my partner's thumbprint.

Now you are ready to
1. Gently place your right thumb on the ink pad.
2. Place your thumb on the piece of paper in a couple of different places. Does your thumbprint look the same as your partner's thumbprint?
3. Wash your hands to get any ink off of them.
4. Use your crayons and markers to make designs around your thumbprints.

Brain exercise
My thumbprint is . . .

Activity Goal	Sensory Note	Key to Success	Hint
To create art around our own unique thumbprints.	We each have our own unique thumbprints.	Adult supervision and protection for clothing will ensure success.	Bright-colored washable ink pads and markers work the best in this activity.

12 Printing Prints Fingerprint Chart

Did you know?
Every one of your fingers has a different fingerprint.

You will need
Play clothes or apron
Fingerprint Chart page 60
Washable colored ink pad
Soap and water

What do you think?
If I make a thumbprint and then make a fingerprint, my thumbprint (will) be or (won't) be the same as my fingerprint.

Now you are ready to
1. Gently place your right thumb on the ink pad.
2. Place your thumb in the first box of the chart.
3. Do the same thing for each finger on your right hand. Can you tell the difference between your fingerprints and your thumbprint?

Brain exercise
All of my fingers have . . .
The fingerprints on the chart are . . .

Activity Goal	Sensory Note	Key to Success	Hint
To display your finger-prints.	Each fingerprint and thumbprint is unique.	Adult supervision and pro-tection for clothing will ensure success. When working with a large group of children, try using a chart made of butcher paper.	The children will enjoy keeping the chart up on a wall for all to see.

Fingerprint Chart

Name	Thumb	Pointer	Middle	Ring	Baby
____					
____					
____					
____					
____					

Did you know?

The mimosa plant will pull back when it is touched.

You will need

Mimosa plant

Lamb's ear plant

Pussywillow branches

What do you think?

I (will) or (won't) be able to make the mimosa pull back when I touch it.

Now you are ready to

1. Gently touch the mimosa plant. What did it do? Why do you think the plant responds to your touch?

2. Touch the lamb's ear. How does it feel? Can you describe the texture?

3. Touch the pussywillows. Are they soft or rough? Try touching one to a spot just above your lips. How did it feel?

4. Which of nature's plants do you like to touch the most?

Brain exercise

When I touched the plants, . . .

Activity Goal	Sensory Note	Key to Success	Hint
To touch the wonders of nature.	Each plant has its own unique texture.	Make sure any plants you share with children are nontoxic and don't cause allergic reactions.	The children enjoy brainstorming plant ideas of their own.

14 What If? No Touch

Did you know?

People who have lost their sense of touch use their other senses to help them make sense of the world.

You will need

Child-size gloves

Egg timer

Grab Box from page 49

What do you think?

If I can't touch things with my fingers, I (will) or (won't) use my other senses to help me.

Now you are ready to

1. Set the timer for 15 minutes.
2. Put on the gloves. You will keep these gloves on until the buzzer rings. See if you can pick up something unbreakable. Try writing with a pencil or marker. Can you identify the objects in the Grab Box?
3. What was it like to be unable to touch things? What happened when you tried to write? Were you able to identify the objects in the Grab Box? What other senses did you use to help you? What dangers might there be if you couldn't feel pain or heat?

Brain exercise

When I couldn't touch things, I . . .

Activity Goal	Sensory Note	Key to Success	Hint
To temporarily experience what life might be like without the ability to feel objects.	A person may lose the sensitivity to touch through loss of limbs, severe burns, or nerve damage.	The gloves need to fit snugly or the activity will be too frustrating for young children.	A stretchy glove (1 size fits all) usually works well for all of the children.

15 Walk About and Touch

Did you know?
Everything around you has its own texture.

You will need
To be outdoors

Blindfold (optional)

What do you think?
If I go outside, I (will) or (won't) be able to tell what I am touching.

Now you are ready to
1. Walk outside with an adult.
2. Put on the blindfold. Let the adult guide you to things that you can safely touch. Try to identify what you are touching. Pay attention to the way the sun or rain feels on your face. Is there any wind? How does it feel when wind blows through your hair? How does your hair feel on your neck or face? Describe what you are feeling.
3. Take off the blindfold. Draw pictures of the things you touched or write about how they felt to you.

Brain exercise
When I walked outside, I could feel . . .

Activity Goal

To explore the different textures in your environment.

Sensory Note

Our fingers will explore shapes and textures to help us identify objects in our environment.

Key to Success

Adult supervision and guidance is necessary.

Hint

If you are unable to go outside, have children explore the fabrics in furniture, the texture of textbooks, and the objects that they find in their classroom or home. When working with a group of children, have them focus on touch without the blindfolds.

All About Smell

My Nose

My nose it knows
How to smell a rose.
My nose it knows
Not to smell my toes.
My nose it knows
Which cookie I chose.

What a smart nose
Have I!

*Sung to "One Little, Two Little,
Three Little Indians"*

In All About Smell you will find

Read All About It!

Author	Title	Publisher
Aliki	*My Five Senses*	HarperCollins, 1989
Monica Byles	*Experiment with Senses*	Lerner Publications, 1994
Allan Fowler	*Rookie Read-About Science Series: Smelling Things*	Childrens Press, 1991
Bruce McMillan	*Sense Suspense: A Guessing Game for the Five Senses*	Scholastic, 1994
Jane Moncure	*What Your Nose Knows*	Childrens Press, 1982
Maria Rius	*The Five Senses Series: Smell*	Barron's, 1985
Cynthia Rylant	*The Relatives Came*	Bradbury Press, 1985
William Steig	*Brave Irene*	Farrar, Straus & Giroux, 1986
Rosemary Wells	*Night Sounds, Morning Colors*	Dial Books, 1994

Smell-Abilities

Why is your sense of smell important?

✪ Your sense of smell gives you information about the world around you. Your brain can distinguish among more than ten thousand smells!

✪ You can smell things most easily when you use your nose to sniff in the vapors of a scent.

✪ If food has spoiled, it smells rotten. Your sense of smell lets you know it shouldn't be eaten. If milk smells sour, you know not to drink it.

✪ Your nose also sends messages to your brain at the same time you chew food. It helps you to taste the food you are eating.

✪ The sense of smell protects you from danger. If you smell smoke, you know that there could be a fire near-by. Your nose can give you information before you even see a fire.

✪ Your brain uses the sense of smell to help you quickly identify the things around you. You know what a flower smells like so you can identify it without even seeing it.

✪ The sense of smell helps you to remember what happened the last time you smelled something. When you smell a certain perfume it may remind you of someone special to you. When you smell a certain food it might remind you of a special holiday. If you smell something that made you sick, you may not want to eat it again.

✪ Some smells make you feel happy, while other smells make you feel sad. The smell of yummy food may make you hungry.

My Sense of Smell Journal

Today I learned

 *Sense-Abilities,* ©1998. Published by Chicago Review Press, Inc., 800-888-7471.

Smell and Guess—Mix and Match

Did you know?
Most things have their own special scent.

You will need
3 very small bowls

Measuring spoons

Lemon, peppermint, and vanilla baking extracts

6 small empty candy-sprinkle jars (or mini-M&M containers)

6 white unscented cotton balls

6 colored circle stickers (2 of each color)

Mix and Match board (optional), page oo, copied onto card stock and laminated if possible

What do you think?
If I smell a lemon scent, I (will) or (won't) be able to match it.

Now you are ready to
1. Measure 1/2 teaspoon of vanilla extract and pour it into one of the small bowls.
2. Pull the plastic top off each of the 6 empty sprinkle jars.
3. Gently dip the bottom of 2 cotton balls into the extract bowl and place them (dipped end first) each into their own jar. Replace the plastic lids and close the jars.
4. Write V for vanilla on 2 stickers of the same color. Put the stickers on the bottoms of the jars with the vanilla-scented cotton balls.
5. Follow steps 1 through 4 for the other extracts.
6. Mix up the jars and see if your nose can match the scents. To use the Mix and Match board, place the matching jars next to each other.

Brain exercise
When I smelled the scented cotton balls, my nose . . .

Activity Goal

To match the scents of 3 extracts.

Sensory Note

We can train our noses to memorize certain scents and then respond when we smell the same scent again.

Key to Success

Using very strong scents inside the jars will help the children to be successful in matching up the scents. Once they have mastered identifying these scents, you can experiment with less pungent scents to challenge their ability to distinguish among them.

Hint

Once your children have mastered this Mix and Match Board, ask them to create their own board and collect scents of their own.

Mix and Match Board

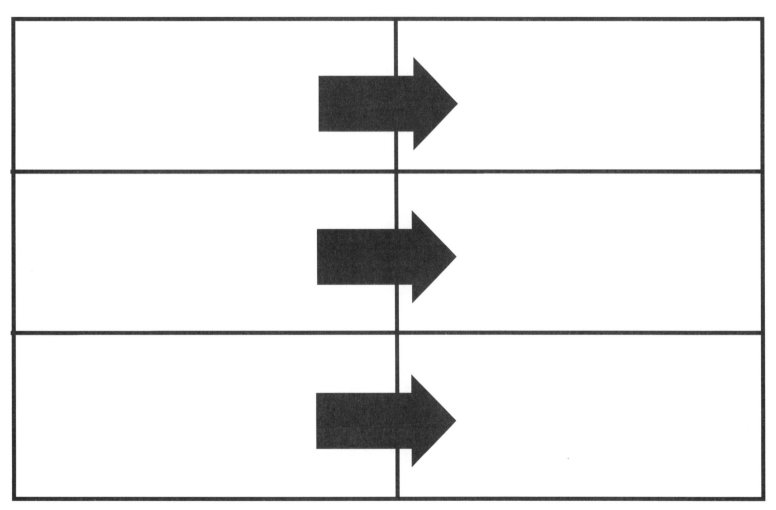

2 What's That Scent? Nose Detectives I

Did you know?
Your sense of smell works much better than your sense of taste.

You will need
At least 5 empty film canisters

Cotton balls

Any 5 of the following (be sure to use the chocolate chips):

   3 large bubble-gum pieces

   1 teaspoon cheese flakes (dip a cotton ball into the flakes)

   1 small broken candy cane (or peppermint extract on a cotton ball)

   Popped popcorn (enough to fill a canister)

   Chocolate chips (enough to fill a canister)

   1 teaspoon peanut butter (use with a cotton ball)

   1 crumbled cookie

   1 teaspoon canned frosting (use with a cotton ball)

   Breakfast cereal (enough to fill a canister)

5 to 9 round stickers, all the same color

Nose Detectives I Things-to-Chew Bingo Board, page 76, copied onto white card stock and laminated if possible

Blindfold (optional)

What do you think?
If I smell inside the canister, I (will) or (won't) be able to match the smell to the picture on the bingo sheet.

Now you are ready to
1. Place each sample in its own canister.
2. Write ND I on enough stickers to label the canisters. Place the stickers on the bottom of the canisters.
3. Set out the Things-to-Chew Bingo Board and mix up the canisters.
4. With your eyes closed or blindfolded, pick up one of the canisters. Open the lid and smell. Shut the lid and place the canister in its matching spot on the Bingo Board.
5. Repeat step 4 with all of the other canisters. See if you can get a 3-in-a-row bingo!

Brain exercise
When I smelled the canisters, my nose . . .

Activity Goal

To identify the scents of things we chew.

Sensory Note

Our noses can distinguish among more than ten thousand different scents.

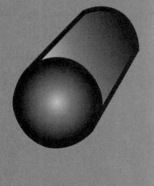

Key to Success

Using familiar scents inside the canisters will help the children to be successful in identifying each scent. Younger children need contextual cues to help them with scent identification. Once children have mastered the Bingo Board, let them mix up the scents and identify them without any cues. Try finding other food scents to test their sense of smell even further. Younger children may have trouble with the canister lids. In this case, substitute mini-M&M containers or punch holes in the canister lids and cover them with masking tape when they are not in use. Adult supervision and guidance is necessary.

Hint

Younger children tend to peek at samples. In this case, a blindfold is helpful. It's a good idea to remind children that this sense is smell, not taste, so it is important not to eat the canister ingredients. *Samples may become rancid in a week or so—check often for freshness.*

Nose Detectives ı Things-to-Chew Bingo Board

Bubble Gum	Cheese	Peppermint
Popcorn	Chocolate	Peanut Butter
Cookies	Cupcake Frosting	Cereal

Sense-Abilities, ©1998. Published by Chicago Review Press, Inc., 800-888-4741.

3 What's That Scent? Nose Detectives II

Did you know?
Even if you recognize a scent you may not be able to name it without other clues.

You will need
Cotton balls

At least 5 empty film canisters

Any 5 or more of the following (be sure to use the Play-Doh):

Baby shampoo (use with a cotton ball)

Cologne or mild perfume (use with a cotton ball)

Pine needles (enough to fill a canister) or pine scent (use with a cotton ball)

Broken crayons (enough to fill a canister)

Play-Doh (enough to fill a canister)

Flower petals (use with a cotton ball)

1 teaspoon ground coffee (use with a cotton ball)

Bath-soap chips (enough to fill a canister)

Toothpaste (use with a cotton ball)

5 to 9 round stickers, all the same color, but choose a different color than you used for ND I

Nose Detectives II Things-at-Home Bingo Board, page 79, copied onto white card stock and laminated if possible

Blindfold (optional)

What do you think?
If I smell inside the canister, I (will) or (won't) be able to match the smell to the picture on the Bingo Board.

Now you are ready to
1. Place each item in its own canister.
2. Write ND II on enough stickers to label the canisters. Place the stickers on the canister bottoms.
3. Set out your Things-at-Home Bingo Board and mix up the canisters.
4. Pick up one of the canisters and close your eyes. Open the lid and smell. Shut the lid and place the canister where you think it fits on the Bingo Board.
5. Repeat step 4 with all of the other canisters. See if you can get a 3-in-a-row bingo!

Brain exercise

When I smelled the Things-at-Home canisters, my nose . . .

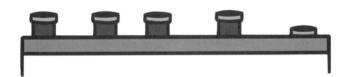

Activity Goal	**Sensory Note**	**Key to Success**	**Hint**
To identify the scents of things usually found at home. 	It is much easier to identify a scent when it is smelled in context. 	Using familiar scents will help the children to be successful in identifying each scent. Younger children need contextual cues to help them in scent identification. Once children have mastered the Bingo Board, let them mix up the scents and identify them without any cues. Try finding other scents at home to test their sense of smell even further.	Some younger children have trouble not peeking when they smell inside the canister. A blindfold can be helpful. You may need to remind children that this sense is smell, not taste, and it is important not to eat the canister ingredients. *The scent samples may become rancid in a week or so—check often for freshness.*

Nose Detectives II Things-at-Home Bingo Board

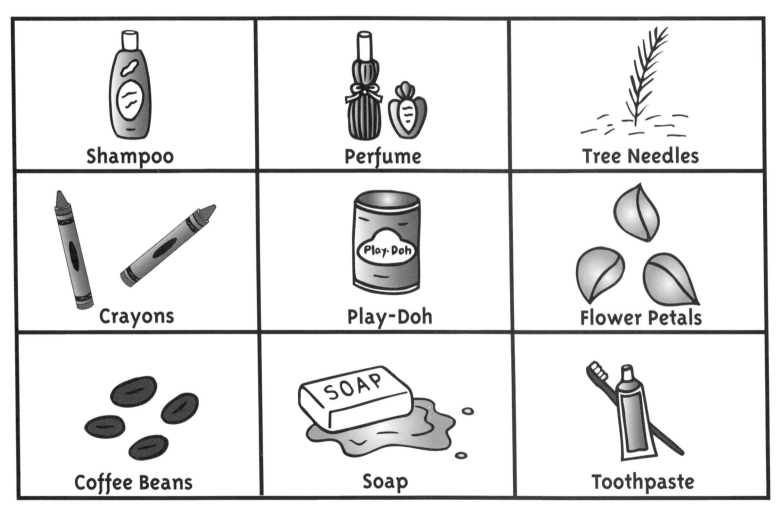

Shampoo	Perfume	Tree Needles
Crayons	Play-Doh	Flower Petals
Coffee Beans	Soap	Toothpaste

Sense-Abilities, ©1998. Published by Chicago Review Press, Inc., 800-888-4741.

4 What's That Scent? Nose Detectives III

Did you know?
Your nose can identify more than ten thousand different scent

You will need
Cotton balls

At least 5 empty film canisters

Any 5 of the following (be sure to use the chocolate chips):

Bacon bits (enough to fill a canister)

Gingerbread crumbs or ground ginger (enough to fill a canister)

Garlic powder (use with a cotton ball)

Butter flakes (use with a cotton ball)

Chocolate chips (enough to fill a canister)

Strawberry extract on a cotton ball (or strawberry-scented candle wax)

Lemon extract or zest (use with a cotton ball)

Dried onion flakes (use with a cotton ball)

Peppercorns (use with a cotton ball)

5 to 9 round stickers (choose a different color than you used for ND I and ND II)

Nose Detectives III Baking Scents Bingo Board, page oo, copied onto white card stock and laminated if possible

Blindfold (optional)

What do you think?
If I smell inside the canister, I (will) or (won't) be able to match the smell to the picture on the Bingo Board.

Now you are ready to
1. Place each item in its own canister.
2. Write ND III on enough of the stickers to label the canisters. Place the stickers on the canister bottoms.
3. Set out your Baking Scents Bingo Board and mix up the canisters.
4. With your eyes closed or blind folded, pick up one of the canisters. Open the lid and smell. Shut the lid and place the canister where you think it fits on the Bingo Board.
5. Repeat step 4 with all the other canisters. See if you can get a 3-in-a-row bingo!

Brain exercise
When I smelled the Baking Scents canisters, my nose . . .

Activity Goal

To identify the scents of things we use when baking.

Sensory Note

We most easily recognize the scents that we smell most often.

Key to Success

Using familiar scents inside the canisters will help the children to be successful in identifying each scent. Younger children need contextual cues to help them with scent identification. Once children have mastered the Bingo Board, let them mix up the scents and identify them without any cues. Try finding other scents used in baking to test their sense of smell even further.

Hint

Some younger children have trouble keeping their eyes closed when they smell inside the canister. A blindfold can be helpful in this case. Remind children that this sense is smell, not taste, so it is important not to eat the canister ingredients. *Samples may become rancid in a week or so—check often for freshness.*

Nose Detectives III Baking Scents Bingo Board

Bacon	Ginger	Garlic
Butter	Chocolate	Strawberries
Lemon	Onion	Pepper

Sense-Abilities, ©1998. Published by Chicago Review Press, Inc., 800-888-4741.

5 Smell and Smile—Scents to Remember

Did you know?
Some scents remind of us places, events, or people in our lives.

You will need
4 empty film canisters

Cotton balls

½ teaspoon pumpkin pie spice (use with a cotton ball)

Popped popcorn (enough to fill a canister)

Chocolate chip cookie crumbs (enough to fill a canister)

Fragrant tree needles (enough to fill a canister)

4 round stickers, all the same color

Smell-and-Smile Bingo Board, page 85, copied onto white card stock and laminated if possible

Blindfold (optional)

What do you think?
If I smell inside the canister, it (will) or (won't) bring back a memory.

Now you are ready to
1. Place each item in a film canister.
2. Write SS on each of the 4 stickers. Place the stickers on the bottoms of the canisters.
3. Set out your Smell-and-Smile Bingo Board and mix up the canisters.
4. With your eyes closed or blindfolded, open the lid and smell the scent inside. Place the canister where you think it fits on the Bingo Board. Does this smell remind you of any event or person? What do you remember when you smell the canister?

Brain exercise
When I smelled inside the canister, I felt . . .

Activity Goal

To link specific scents to a memory.

Sensory Note

There is a strong connection between certain scents and memories. Pumpkin reminds some children of Thanksgiving and ginger reminds some of gingerbread cookies. Popcorn makes many people think of the movies. One child said that the smell of pizza reminds him of his grandfather because they always eat pizza together.

Key to Success

Think about what smells might be linked to events for your children. If possible, use these scents in the canisters. Ask your children to describe the memory that is linked to the scent.

Hint

Once children have mastered this Bingo Board, ask them to create their own board and collect their own scents.

Smell-and-Smile Bingo Board

6 Snoozing on the Job? Nose Doze

Did you know?
Your nose goes to sleep after it has smelled the same scent for awhile.

You will need
Cinnamon stick

Scissors

Old shoelace or piece of cord

Empty film canister with lid

What do you think?
If I wear a cinnamon-stick necklace, I (will) or (won't) be able to smell it at all times.

Now you are ready to
1. Break the cinnamon stick into short segments that can be strung onto a shoelace.
2. String the cinnamon-stick segments so that they fit into the middle of the shoelace.
3. Tie the shoelace around your neck to form a necklace.
4. Raise your hand when you first realize that you don't smell the necklace anymore.
5. Let someone else try wearing the necklace.
6. When you are finished with this activity, place the necklace back into the canister and close the lid to keep the scent fresh.

Brain exercise
After wearing the cinnamon necklace for awhile, . . .

Activity Goal

To show how the nose accommodates to a scent.

Sensory Note

Our brains need to attend to many things. Once a scent is noted it goes into the background so that our brains can attend to new information.

Key to Success

Make sure the necklace is short enough to be close to the nose, but long enough to fall upon clothing, not skin. Get back to everyday activities while the necklace is being worn.

Hint

It can take quite a while before the scent is no longer apparent to the child.

7 Make a Lemon-Scented Memory

You will need

5 cups very cold water

1 cup sugar

Enough lemons to make 1 cup lemon juice

Lemon squeezer

Measuring cup

Large pitcher

Knife

Small paper cups

Makes 6–7 cups of lemonade

Now you are ready to

1. Pour the 5 cups water into the pitcher.
2. Add sugar.
3. Stir until the sugar is dissolved in the water.
4. Cut the lemons in half and squeeze the until you have 1 cup lemon juice. (Save the lemon rinds.)
5. Add the lemon juice to the sugar-water mixture.
6. Stir it all together and pour it into individual cups.
7. Cut the lemon rinds into enough pieces so that everyone gets a piece.
8. Smell the lemon rind. Does it smell like the lemonade?
9. Remember the smells and the fun you've had today.

Activity Goal	Sensory Note	Key to Success	Hint
To create a memory around a scent.	The more senses involved in the activity, the more powerful the memory will be.	Make sure that clothing is protected and lemony fingers don't rub eyes, or your memories may not be positive.	Buy a lemon a few weeks after the lemonade-making activity. Ask the children to smell the lemon and tell you if it brings to mind any memories.

8 Gingernose! Smelly Cookies

You will need

1 1/4 cups flour

1/4 teaspoon baking soda

1/2 teaspoon ground ginger

1/8 teaspoon allspice

1/4 teaspoon salt

1/4 cup canola oil

1/4 cup brown sugar

1/4 cup dark molasses

1/8 cup water

2 bowls, 1 small and 1 large

Electric mixer

Plastic wrap

Refrigerator

Rolling pin

Oven

Bell-shaped cookie cutters
(flat bottom and no clapper),
strawberry-shaped cookie
cutter

Knife

Spatula

Cookie sheets

Shortening or canola oil for
greasing the cookie sheets

Wire rack

*Makes approximately 2 1/2 dozen
small nose cookies*

89

Now you are ready to

1. Measure and mix the flour, baking soda, ginger, allspice, and salt together in the small bowl.
2. Blend the canola oil and brown sugar together in the large bowl using an electric mixer.
3. Pour the molasses and water into the sugar mixture and blend.
4. Stir the flour mixture into the sugar mixture.
5. Cover the large bowl holding the cookie dough with plastic wrap and place it in the refrigerator overnight.
6. Set oven for 375°.
7. Roll out the gingerbread dough on a lightly floured board to a thickness of about ¼ inch.
8. Using a bell-shaped cookie cutter, cut out a cookie. Use the knife to cut it in half. Each half becomes the shape of a nose in profile.
9. Use a spatula to place each nose cookie onto a greased cookie sheet.
10. Bake the cookies for 10 minutes.
11. Place them on a wire rack to cool.
12. You can frost the nose cookies or eat them plain. Either way they smell great and taste delicious.

Activity Goal	Sensory Note	Key to Success	Hint
To make nose-shaped cookies with a strong scent.	When we smell individual ingredients, we can then predict which scent will be the most powerful.	Identify safety hazards and specific rules for working in a kitchen. Give each child an opportunity to cut out a cookie. You could even make a cookie chart so each child gets to eat the cookie he/she cut out.	If you don't have time to involve the children in the initial preparation, start at step 6. If you don't have access to an oven, refrigerate the prepared cookies and bake them later.

9 Cinnamon-Scented Fun—Sweet Heart Magnet

You will need

Makes approximately 10 heart magnets, depending on their size

1 cup ground cinnamon

1 cup applesauce

1 teaspoon allspice

Mixing bowl

Teaspoon

Measuring cup

Wooden spoon

Rolling pin

Heart-shaped cookie cutters

Newspaper

Spatula

Glue

Glitter

Scissors

Magnet with a self-adhesive strip

Now you are ready to

1. Measure and mix the cinnamon, applesauce, and all-spice together in the bowl.

2. Roll out the dough on a flat surface to a thickness of about ¼ inch.

3. Using the heart-shaped cookie cutter, cut out individual hearts.

4. Open up a sheet of newspaper. Use a spatula to place each heart on the newspaper.

5. Let the hearts air-dry for about 4 days, turning them once every day.

6. Decorate the hearts with glue and glitter (optional). Cut the magnet to fit on the back of the heart. Take the protective paper from the magnet's self-adhesive strip and press the magnet firmly on the back of the heart.

7. Place the heart magnet on your refrigerator or give it to someone special as a present.

Activity Goal	Sensory Note	Key to Success	Hint
To create a scented magnet.	All of us have favorite scents. Cinnamon is a favorite scent of young children.	It may be easier for very young children to make an undecorated heart.	Relatives love getting these hearts as gifts. The same recipe works well for all types of ornaments. Just use a coffee stirrer or straw to make a hole at the top.

10 Things I Love to Smell Card Book

You will need

Paper or card stock

Crayons and markers

Pencil

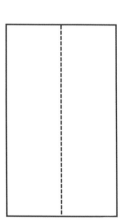 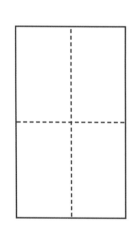 

Now you are ready to

1. Fold a sheet of paper in half.

2. Open it up and fold it in half again.

3. Using the folded edge as the top, fold the paper into a card shape.

4. On the cover write My Smell Book by (your name) and draw a picture of yourself.

5. On the other pages, draw pictures of your favorite scents.

6. Share your book with your friends.

Activity Goal	Sensory Note	Key to Success	Hint
To make a simple book on the sense of smell.	Smelling a number of the samples used in other activities helps children select their smells.	Younger children may need you to fold the card books ahead of time so they can focus on recording their favorite.	This card-book idea is fun, simple, and can be used for each of the senses.

II Nature and Me—My Scented Garden

You will need

Small plastic seed trays

Clay flowerpot

Potting soil

Old newspapers

Big spoon

Rosemary seeds

Lavender seeds

Corsican mint seeds

Lemon-grass seeds

Hyacinth bulb or narcissus bulb

Watering can

Water

Sunny window

Now you are ready to

1. Fill the seed trays and the clay pot ¾ full with potting soil, spreading old newspapers underneath to catch the spills.
2. Use the spoon to dig out spots for the seeds in the seed trays and for the bulb in the clay pot.
3. Sprinkle the seeds and push the bulb down into the dirt.
4. Cover the seeds and bulb with potting soil.
5. Water all the seeds and the bulb and place the trays and pot in a sunny spot.
6. Remember to keep the plants in a sunny spot and keep them watered.
7. Once the seeds and bulb have grown into plants, enjoy their special scents.

Activity Goal

To grow plants with wonderful scents.

Sensory Note

Herbs are nontoxic and have wonderful strong scents.

Key to Success

Select plants that will grow easily inside. Learn as much as you can about the care of these plants so they will thrive under the care of your young botanists.

Hint

This activity can be messy. Use plenty of newspaper underneath the seed trays and clay pot, and be prepared for some cleanup. In the long run, this garden of aromatic delights will be well worth your effort.

12 What If? No Smell!

Did you know?
People who can't smell have a difficult time tasting food.

You will need
Child-size noseplugs (optional)

Egg timer

What do you think?
If my nose is plugged, I (will) or (won't) be able to smell things as I usually do.

Now you are ready to
1. Set the timer for 10 minutes.
2. With an adult's help, place the noseplugs on your nose and continue your activities. When the timer rings, take off the noseplugs.
3. Think about how it felt without your sense of smell. Did you try to eat something? What senses would you use if you couldn't smell a fire or tell if food was bad? How would your other senses help you?

Brain exercise
When I couldn't smell, . . .

Activity Goal	Sensory Note	Key to Success	Hint
To temporarily experience what life might be like without the sense of smell.	If our ability to smell is compromised, we are limited in identifying the objects around us and potential dangers such as spoiled food and fire.	Some children may be uncomfortable breathing out of their mouths. If so, let them hold their noses briefly and try to smell to achieve the same affect.	To save time and effort, select previously prepared materials from other activities in this chapter. You can use everyday items from your home or classroom.

13 Walk About and Smell

Did you know?
Smells are all around you everywhere you go.

You will need
To be outdoors or inside in a new place
Blindfold

What do you think?
If I go outside, I (will) or (won't) be able to smell the scents of nature.

Now you are ready to
1. Walk outside and sniff the air. What do you smell?
2. Sit in one spot. Put on the blindfold. Do the smells change? Do you recognize the smells?
3. Take off the blindfold. Draw pictures or write about the things that you could smell.

Brain exercise
When I walked outside, I could smell . . .

Activity Goal	Sensory Note	Key to Success	Hint
To explore the scents in our environment.	Sometimes we need to take a moment and smell the flowers.	Adult supervision is vital to the success of this activity.	If it is too cold or wet to go outside, try going to an indoor market or explore some other location filled with scents.

98

All About Taste

My Tongue

I have a tongue with taste buds
So when I eat
I know if my food is bitter
Or sweet.

My tongue can tell salty
From sour too.
It tells me what
I like to chew!

Sung to "I'm a Little Teapot"

In All About Taste you will find

Read All About It!

Author	Title	Publisher
Aliki	*My Five Senses*	HarperCollins, 1989
Monica Byles	*Experiment with Senses*	Lerner Publications, 1994
Allan Fowler	*Rookie Read-About Science Series: Tasting Things*	Childrens Press, 1991
B.G. Hennessy	*Jake Baked the Cake*	Viking, 1990
Bruce McMillan	*Sense Suspense: A Guessing Game for the Five Senses*	Scholastic, 1994
Ann Morris	*Share Bread, Bread, Bread*	Morrow, 1993
Patricia Pollacco	*Thunder Cake*	Philomel, 1990
Maria Rius	*The Five Senses Series: Taste*	Barron's, 1985
Cynthia Rylant	*The Relatives Came*	Bradbury Press, 1985
William Steig	*Brave Irene*	Farrar, Straus & Giroux, 1986
Tobi Tobias	*Pot Luck*	Lothrop, 1993
Rosemary Wells	*Night Sounds, Morning Colors*	Dial Books, 1994

Taste-Abilities

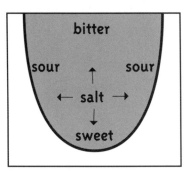

bitter
sour · sour
← salt →
sweet

Why is your sense of taste important?

✪ Your tongue is covered with about ten thousand tiny taste buds that tell you what flavor you are tasting.

✪ You have more taste buds than an adult does.

✪ Your sense of taste gives you information about whether a food tastes bitter like coffee, sweet like oranges, sour like lemons, or salty like pretzels.

✪ Taste buds that recognize bitter flavors are usually found in the back of your tongue. Sour tastes are usually identified by taste buds on the sides of your tongue. The taste buds that identify salty foods are found all over your tongue. Most of the taste buds for recognizing sweet flavors are found right at the tip of your tongue. There are also some taste buds on the inner surface of your cheeks and the roof of your mouth.

✪ The liquid in your mouth is called saliva. Saliva mixes with your food and makes it possible for you to taste it. If your tongue is dry you can't taste the food you are eating.

✪ You also need the sense of smell to taste food. The smell of the food you are eating goes right up your nose when you are eating it. Your senses of smell and taste work together to give you information about the flavor.

✪ You are able to determine which food you are eating by how crunchy, gooey, chewy, mushy, crisp, soft, or hard it is. You know that apples off the tree have a certain flavor but also taste crisp and sound crunchy when you eat them. Oatmeal tastes very mushy and is chewy in its own way. You know that peanut butter sticks to the roof of your mouth. Your lips, mouth, tongue, and teeth each give you information about the food you are eating.

✪ Your tongue is not very sensitive to temperature. Sometimes you don't know that you're drinking something that is too hot until you have burned your tongue. So it is important to check the temperature of things you will be drinking before you drink them.

My Sense of Taste Journal

Today I learned

Bumpy Tongue? Taste Buds' Delight

Did you know?

Your tongue has taste buds all over it to help you pick out the different flavors of the foods you eat.

You will need

Partner

Plenty of light

Magnifying glass for a closer look (optional)

What do you think?

If I look at my partner's tongue, I (will) or (won't) be able to see lots of bumps that contain taste buds.

Now you are ready to

1. When your partner is ready to observe, open up your mouth and stick out your tongue.
2. Give your partner some time to make scientific observations. What did your partner see?
3. Ask your partner to stick out his/her tongue. What do you see?
4. Did you see the same things? Are your tongues shiny?
5. If you want a closer look, use a magnifying glass.

Brain exercise

My partner's tongue . . .

Activity Goal	Sensory Note	Key to Success	Hint
To look more closely at the tongue.	Our tongues are covered with about ten thousand taste buds.	Make sure the room has very good lighting.	Sometimes children need to be reminded that they are scientists so they focus on learning about their tongues instead of sticking out their tongues.

2 What's That Taste? Taste Detectives I

Did you know?
The taste buds on your tongue can tell when you taste something sweet.

You will need
Gummy bear for each child

Napkin for each child

What do you think?
If I taste a gummy bear, my tongue (will) or (won't) be able to tell its flavor.

Now you are ready to
1. Look at the gummy bear. How do you think it will taste?
2. Touch the gummy bear to the tip of your tongue. How does it taste?
3. Touch the gummy bear on the side of your tongue. Does it taste the same or different?
4. Place the gummy bear in the middle of your tongue. Has the taste changed?
5. Slowly chew the gummy bear. Note the texture. Is it crunchy? Is it slippery? Is it chewy?
6. Does the texture of the gummy bear change when you eat it? Does its flavor change?
7. Where on your tongue was the taste of the gummy bear the strongest?

Brain exercise
When I tasted the gummy bear, my tongue told me . . .

Activity Goal	Sensory Note	Key to Success	Hint
To identify a sweet flavor and note the location of taste buds sensitive to that flavor.	The taste buds for sweet flavors are generally found at the tip of the tongue. However, each individual is unique and your children may find their flavor sensitivities in different locations.	When children approach this activity as scientists, they see themselves conducting research and making scientific observations.	Gummy bears are easily accessible and the children love them. If you would rather use a naturally sweet food, try apple slices or slices of some other fruit.

3 What's That Taste? Taste Detectives II

Did you know?
The taste buds on your tongue can tell when you taste something salty.

You will need
Salted pretzel stick for each child

Napkin for each child

What do you think?
If I taste a pretzel, my tongue (will) or (won't) be able to tell its flavor.

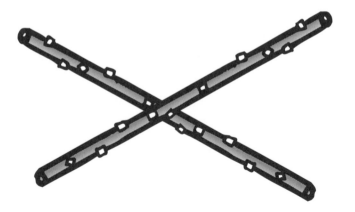

Now you are ready to
1. Look at the pretzel. How do you think it will taste?
2. Touch the pretzel to the tip of your tongue. How does it taste?
3. Touch the pretzel on the side of your tongue. Does it taste the same or different?
4. Place the pretzel in the middle of your tongue. Has the taste changed?
5. Slowly chew the pretzel. Note the texture. Is it crunchy? Is it slippery? Is it chewy?
6. Does the texture of the pretzel change when you eat it? Does its flavor change?
7. Where on your tongue was the taste of the pretzel strongest?

Brain exercise
When I tasted the pretzel, I . . .

Activity Goal

To identify a salty flavor and note the location of taste buds sensitive to that flavor.

Sensory Note

The taste buds for salty flavors are generally found all over the tongue. However, each individual is unique and your children may find their flavor sensitivities in different locations.

Key to Success

When children approach this activity as scientists, they see themselves conducting research and making scientific observations.

Hint

Pretzels are easily accessible and the children love them. Table salt works well too.

4 What's That Taste? Taste Detectives III

Did you know?
The taste buds on your tongue can tell when you taste something sour.

You will need
Sour Patch Kids candy for each child

Napkin for each child

What do you think?
If I taste a Sour Patch Kids candy, my tongue (will) or (won't) be able to tell its flavor.

Now you are ready to
1. Look at the Sour Patch Kids candy. How do you think it will taste?
2. Touch the candy to the tip of your tongue. How does it taste?
3. Touch the candy on the side of your tongue. Does it taste the same or different?
4. Place the candy in the middle of your tongue. Has the taste changed?
5. Slowly chew the candy. Note the texture. Is it crunchy? Is it slippery? Is it chewy?
6. Does the texture of the candy change when you eat it? Does its flavor change?
7. Where on your tongue was the taste of the Sour Patch Kids candy strongest?

Brain exercise
When I tasted the Sour Patch Kids candy, my tongue told me . . .

Activity Goal

To identify a sour flavor and note the location of taste buds sensitive to that flavor.

Sensory Note

The taste buds for sour flavors are generally found on the sides of the tongue. However, each individual is unique and your children may find their flavor sensitivities in different locations.

Key to Success

When children approach this activity as scientists, they see themselves conducting research and making scientific observations.

Hint

Sour Patch Kids candy is found in most grocery stores. Fresh lemon slices are a natural alternative and work very well.

5 What's That Taste? Taste Detectives IV

Did you know?
The taste buds on your tongue can tell when you taste something bitter.

You will need
Grated unsweetened chocolate (decaffeinated instant coffee crystals may also be used)

Napkin for each child

What do you think?
If I taste unsweetened chocolate, my tongue (will) or (won't) be able to tell its flavor.

Now you are ready to
1. Look at the unsweetened chocolate. How do you think it will taste?
2. Touch the unsweetened chocolate to the tip of your tongue. How does it taste?
3. Touch the unsweetened chocolate on the side of your tongue. Does it taste the same or different?
4. Place the unsweetened chocolate in the middle of your tongue. Has the taste changed?
5. Slowly chew the unsweetened chocolate. Note the texture. Is it crunchy? Is it slippery? Is it chewy?
6. Does the texture of the unsweetened chocolate change when you eat it? Does its flavor change?
7. Where on your tongue was the taste of the unsweetened chocolate strongest?

Brain exercise
When I tasted the unsweetened chocolate, . . .

Activity Goal

To identify a bitter flavor and note the location of taste buds sensitive to that flavor.

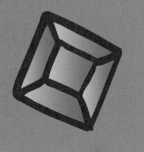

Sensory Note

The taste buds for bitter flavors are generally found toward the back of the tongue. However, each individual is unique and your children may find their flavor sensitivities in different locations.

Key to Success

When children approach this activity as scientists, they see themselves conducting research and making scientific observations. Most children disliked the flavor and used their napkins to remove the unsweetened chocolate from their mouths. However, some children couldn't tell it from sweetened chocolate and asked for more.

Hint

Unsweetened chocolate is easily accessible. Instant coffee crystals may also be used to identify bitter tastes.

6 Liquid Clues—Juicy Treats

Did you know?
You are very good at identifying the flavor of both foods and drinks.

For each person tasting, you will need
Blindfold

Partner

Lemonade without pulp in small paper cup

Orange juice without pulp in small paper cup

Apple juice in small paper cup

Napkin

What do you think?
If I taste lemonade, I (will) or (won't) be able to identify it.

Now you are ready to
1. Put on the blindfold.
2. Ask your partner to hand you a cup of juice.
3. Drink the juice and identify what kind you think it is.
4. Follow steps 2 and 3 with the other 2 cups of juice.
5. How many times were you right?
6. If your partner wants to guess, just repeat steps 1 through 5.

Brain exercise
When I tasted the different kinds of juice, my tongue . . .

Activity Goal

To identify a flavor just by taste.

Sensory Note

When we are determining what type of food we are eating, we take many different characteristics into consideration. In this activity, the taster focuses mainly on the taste, not the shape, sound, or texture of the food.

Key to Success

Using familiar juices will help the children to be successful in identifying each taste. Younger children may need contextual cues to help them with taste identification. If this is the case with your children, let them identify each sample by pointing to its carton instead of using words. Once the children have mastered these tastes, try challenging them by serving grapefruit juice, orange juice, and lemonade together in a taste test.

Hint

This activity requires adult supervision.

7 Match a Taste—Tongue Ticklers

Did you know?

You only need to taste a small portion of food or drink to match it to the same flavor. When you taste a carbonated drink, it tickles your tongue.

For each person tasting, you will need

Marker

4 circle stickers

2 small paper cups with 3 tablespoons of 7-Up in each

2 small paper cups with 3 tablespoons of ginger ale in each

Taste and Match sheet

Napkin

What do you think?

If I taste 7-Up and ginger ale, I (will) or (won't) be able to tell the difference.

Now you are ready to

1. With the marker, write 7 and G on each of 2 stickers to total 4 stickers per person. Place the stickers on the bottoms of the cups of pop that start with that letter.

2. Carefully mix up the cups so that you don't know what is in each cup.

3. Using the Taste and Match sheet, drink a bit of the pop in one cup and place it on the left.

4. Sip from each cup until you find the taste that matches the taste of the first pop. When you think you have a match, place the matching cup to the right of the first cup.

5. Repeat steps 3 and 4 with the rest of your pop samples.

6. When you are finished, lift each cup up to see if the stickers match. How did you do?

Brain exercise

When I tasted the different flavors, . . .

Activity Goal

To match 2 different flavors to themselves.

Sensory Note

When tasting liquids with similar textures, we identify them by their flavor only.

Key to Success

Use only a small portion of pop in each cup. If this activity is too difficult for your children, try using very different-tasting drinks to help them be successful. For more of a challenge, use Sprite in place of ginger ale, or try two different colas.

Hint

Use only a small portion of pop in each cup. If you prefer to avoid pop, try using different types of sparkling ciders instead.

8 No Smell? No Taste!

Did you know?
You can't taste things without your sense of smell.

You will need
Blindfold

Bag of dried apple or banana chips

What do you think?
If I taste a fruit chip without smelling it, I (will) or (won't) be able to identify the flavor.

Now you are ready to
1. Put on the blindfold.
2. Pull a chip out of the bag.
3. Hold your nose and taste the chip. Can you tell what it is?
4. Taste the chip without holding your nose. How does it taste?

Brain exercise
When I tried to taste the chip without smelling it, . . .

Activity Goal	Sensory Note	Key to Success	Hint
To experience the importance of the sense of smell when we taste food.	Some experts believe that at least 80 percent of our experience of taste actually comes from the sense of smell.	If a child has a cold, it may hinder his/her ability to be successful with this activity.	Dried fruit chips work well since most other foods are too easily identified by touch. Fresh apple and raw potato slices can also be used.

9 Dry Tongue? No Fun!

Did you know?
Your tongue needs saliva to taste different flavors.

You will need
Clean paper towel for each child

Wastebasket

Sugar cube for each child

Drinking fountain nearby or small cups of water

What do you think?
If I touch a sugar cube to the tip of my dry tongue, I (will) or (won't) be able to taste the sugar.

Now you are ready to
1. Use a paper towel to pat-dry the tip of your tongue.
2. Touch a sugar cube to the tip of your tongue. Can you taste anything?
3. Place the sugar cube on your tongue. Wait for a minute until your tongue replenishes the saliva.
4. What did the sugar cube taste like after your tongue became moist again? What shape did it feel like? How did the texture change as you ate it?

Brain exercise
When I tasted a sugar cube with a dry tongue, . . .

Activity Goal	Sensory Note	Key to Success	Hint
To recognize the importance of saliva to the sense of taste.	Saliva mixes with food and brings the flavor to our taste buds. It also aids in the digestion of food.	Make sure that the children don't dry too far back. You wouldn't want to elicit the gag reflex.	Some children may not be comfortable doing this activity. They can observe someone else and learn the same information.

10 Terrific Textures—Talented Tongue

Did you know?
The different textures of the foods you eat help you to identify them.

You will need
Partner

Blindfold(s)

Small plastic spoons

Food samples in small paper cups:

Cooked oatmeal (mushy)

Croutons (crunchy)

Graham crackers dipped in applesauce (soggy)

Celery sticks (chewy)

Applesauce (soft)

Carrot sticks (crisp)

Small hard candies

What do you think?
If I taste cooked oatmeal, I (will) or (won't) know its texture and be able to identify it.

Now you are ready to
1. Choose a partner and ask him/her to put on the blindfold.
2. Have your partner taste the first sample. What does he/she think it is? Ask him/her to describe the texture and the noise it makes.
3. Now it's your turn to put on the blindfold.
4. Taste the second sample. What do you think it is? Tell your partner about the texture and noise it makes.
5. Repeat steps 1 through 3 until you've gone through all the samples. How well did you both identify the textures and foods?

Brain exercise
When I tasted a sample, my tongue knew . . .

Activity Goal	Sensory Note	Key to Success	Hint
To identify foods by both their taste and their texture.	When we identify foods, we pay attention to taste, shape, and texture. These factors influence our food choices.	This exercise requires adult help. It can be messy—aprons may be appropriate.	Small sample spoons like the ones you find at ice-cream parlors work very well with this activity. If you are working with a large group, ask several children at a time to taste one food or drink sample. Then have several more children taste the next food or juice sample until all samples have been tested.

11 Try a New Taste—Whoopee!

Did you know?

As you grow older, the flavors you like to eat may change.

You will need

Partner

Blindfold

Small plastic spoons

Napkins

Food and drink samples in small paper cups (use very small portions):

Tomato juice

Prune juice

Black olive slices

Grapefruit juice

Fresh mushroom slices

Pitted dates

Raw cauliflower

What do you think?

If I taste prune juice, I (will) or (won't) like the way it tastes.

Now you are ready to

1. Taste each juice.
2. Taste each food.
3. What was your favorite food? What was your favorite juice?
   Was there anything you didn't like?
4. Talk to your friends about what they liked and didn't like.

Brain exercise

When I tasted a new taste sample, my tongue . . .

Activity Goal

To try out new tastes.

Sensory Note

Children have more taste buds than adults. Their tastes will change as they grow older.

Key to Success

This exercise requires adult help. It can be messy—aprons may be appropriate.

Hint

If you are working with a large group, ask several children at a time to taste one food or drink sample. Then have several more children taste the next food or juice sample until all samples have been tested.

Fantastic Flavor! Sensational Snickerdoodles

You will need

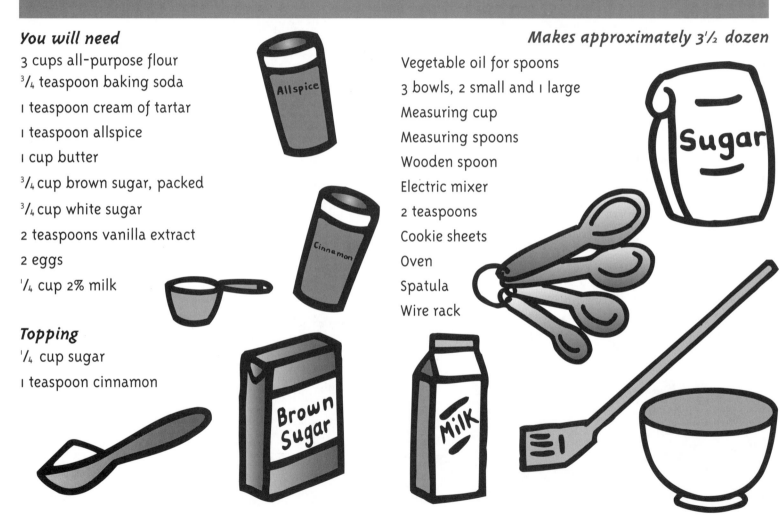

3 cups all-purpose flour

$^3/_4$ teaspoon baking soda

1 teaspoon cream of tartar

1 teaspoon allspice

1 cup butter

$^3/_4$ cup brown sugar, packed

$^3/_4$ cup white sugar

2 teaspoons vanilla extract

2 eggs

$^1/_4$ cup 2% milk

Topping

$^1/_4$ cup sugar

1 teaspoon cinnamon

Makes approximately 3$^1/_2$ dozen

Vegetable oil for spoons

3 bowls, 2 small and 1 large

Measuring cup

Measuring spoons

Wooden spoon

Electric mixer

2 teaspoons

Cookie sheets

Oven

Spatula

Wire rack

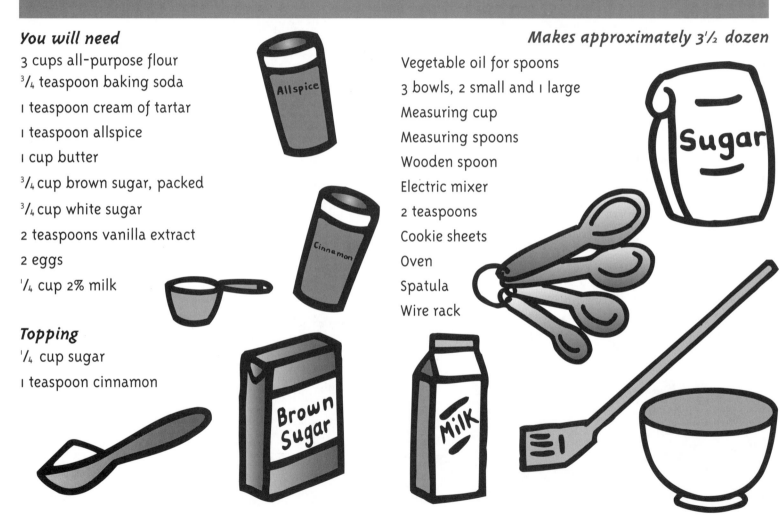

Now you are ready to

1. Measure and mix the flour, baking soda, cream of tartar, and allspice together in a small bowl. Set aside. In the other small bowl, mix the cinnamon and sugar for the topping. Set this aside too.

2. Using an electric mixer, blend the butter, sugars, and vanilla together in the large bowl.

3. Beat in the eggs. Then, still using the mixer, add the milk and the flour mixture.

4. Use 2 oiled teaspoons to make each cookie. Dip one teaspoon into the batter and use the other to scrape it off the first spoon and place it onto a cookie sheet.

5. Sprinkle each cookie with the cinnamon-sugar topping.

6. Bake cookies in a preheated oven at 375° about 10 minutes (until golden brown).

7. While the cookies are still warm, use a spatula to loosen them from the cookie sheet.

8. Place them on a wire rack to cool.

13 Nature and Me—Natural Sweets

Did you know?
Some of the sweetest flavors come from nature.

You will need
Partner

Thin latex gloves for each child
(optional; check for latex allergies)

Blindfold

Fresh fruit samples:

  Orange slices

  Apple slices

  Coconut pieces

  Pineapple chunks

Paper napkins

Paper towels

What do you think?
If I taste something from nature, I (will) or (won't)
know its name.

Now you are ready to
1. Choose a partner to work with you. Ask your partner
   to put on the blindfold. Put on your gloves.
2. Feed your partner the first sample. What does
   he/she think it is? Ask your partner to describe the
   texture and shape.
3. Now switch with your partner as you put on the
   blindfold and your partner puts on gloves to feed
   you the next sample.
4. Taste the second sample. What texture and shape is
   it? What do you think it is?
5. Repeat steps 1 through 4 until you've gone through
   all the samples. How well did you both identify the
   foods from nature?

Brain exercise
When I tasted a sample from nature, I . . .

Activity Goal

To identify natural foods by both their taste and texture.

Sensory Note

Children will use their sense of smell and their ability to decipher taste, texture, and shape to identify each food sample.

Key to Success

This activity can be a bit sticky. Make sure you have plenty of paper towels.

Hint

Thin latex gloves are great—they make this activity virus-free. Make sure that no one is allergic to latex and that children don't inadvertently bite their partners.

14 What If? No Taste!

Did you know?
People who have no sense of taste use their other senses to help them know more about what they are eating.

You will need
Child-size noseplugs

Timer

Lunch

What do you think?
If I can't taste or smell, I (will) or (won't) enjoy eating my food.

Now you are ready to
1. Set the timer for 10 minutes.
2. With an adult's help, place the noseplugs on your nose and eat your lunch.
3. What was it like to be unable to smell or taste your food? How did you feel when others were enjoying their lunch? Was it harder to tell what you were eating? What other senses did you use to help you? What dangers might there be if you couldn't tell what you were eating?

Brain exercise
When I couldn't taste my food, I . . .

Activity Goal	Sensory Note	Key to Success	Hint
To temporarily experience what it might be like to live without the senses of smell and taste.	If we cannot taste our food we lose an important part of our eating experience.	Make sure the noseplugs fit snugly yet comfortably.	Lunch or snacktimes are perfect for this exercise. Noseplugs need to be sanitized after each use.

15 Walk About a Kitchen

Did you know?
Smell is an important part of eating.

You will need
Kitchen where food is cooking or baking

Blindfold

What do you think?
If I go into a kitchen full of good food smells, I (will) or (won't) be hungry.

Now you are ready to
1. Walk into the kitchen and sniff the aroma. What do you smell? Does it make your mouth water?
2. Sit in one spot. Put on the blindfold. Do the smells change? Do you recognize the smells? Do they make you hungry? Ask to taste-test a food. Was it tasty?
3. Take off the blindfold. Draw pictures or write about the things you smelled and tasted.

Brain exercise
When I walked into that kitchen, my . . .

Activity Goal	Sensory Note	Key to Success	Hint
To explore the aromas and tastes in a kitchen.	The sense of smell is an important component in enjoying the foods we eat.	Adult supervision is vital to the success of this activity.	Wait until there is enough room in the kitchen to really explore this subject comfortably. With large groups of children it is fun to schedule a trip to the school cafeteria. No blindfolds are necessary.

All About Hearing

My Ears

They are listening!
They are listening!
My two ears, my two ears.

Sounds are all around me
Their vibrations found me.
Through the air.
Through the air.

Sung to "Are You Sleeping?"

132

In All About Hearing you will find

Read All About It!

Author	Title	Publisher
Aliki	*My Five Senses*	HarperCollins, 1989
Arlene Blanchard	*Sounds My Feet Make*	Random House, 1988
Monica Byles	*Experiment with Senses*	Lerner Publications, 1994
Rebecca Emberly	*City Sounds*	Little, Brown, 1989
Allan Fowler	*Rookie Read-About Science Series: Hearing Things*	Childrens Press, 1991
Helen Griffith	*Georgia Music*	Greenwillow Books, 1986
Rachel Isadora	*I Hear*	Greenwillow Books, 1985
Patricia MacLaclan	*Through Grandpa's Eyes*	Harper and Row, 1980
Bruce McMillan	*Sense Suspense: A Guessing Game for the Five Senses*	Scholastic, 1994
Mary Beth Mill	*Handtalk School*	Four Winds Press, 1991
Mildred Pitts	*Ty's One-Man Band*	Four Winds Press, 1980
Laura Rankin	*The Handmade Alphabet*	Dial Books, 1991
Maria Rius	*The Five Senses Series: Hearing*	Barron's, 1985
Cynthia Rylant	*The Relatives Came*	Bradbury Press, 1985
Erica Silverman	*Don't Fidget a Feather*	Macmillan, 1994
Rosemary Wells	*Night Sounds, Morning Colors*	Dial Books, 1994

Hearing-Abilities

Why is your sense of hearing important?

✪ Sounds are vibrations. Vibrations are like waves going through the air. They are caused by movement. The movement of an object creates ripples all around it.

✪ Your eardrum is a tightly stretched piece of thin skin. It is stretched across the end of your ear canal. Sound vibrations come into your ear through this canal and push against your eardrum.

✪ Your ears are shaped to funnel sound waves into your ear canals so that sound will reach your eardrum and vibrate the three small bones on the opposite side. These bones are called the hammer, the anvil, and the stirrup.

✪ The vibrations from the three tiny bones pass to a snail-shaped tube (cochlea) filled with liquid. It has thousands of special hairlike nerve cells that turn the vibrations into messages to the brain.

✪ One of the most important things our ears do for us is to help us keep our balance. Fluid in the three semicircular canals helps us maintain our balance.

✪ Vibrations can travel through other materials (like telephone wires) to reach your ears.

✪ Animals hear more sounds than people. Children can usually hear better than adults.

✪ Almost everything on earth can make sound. Sound travels through the air at 1,100 feet per second. Sound travels much slower than light. This is why you see lightning first and then hear the thunder it causes. Sound travels four times faster through water than air.

✪ Loud noises can harm our ears and affect our sense of hearing forever. Be sure to protect your ears from very loud sounds.

✪ There is a special language called American Sign Language (page 137) for people who can't hear speech.

Inside the Ear

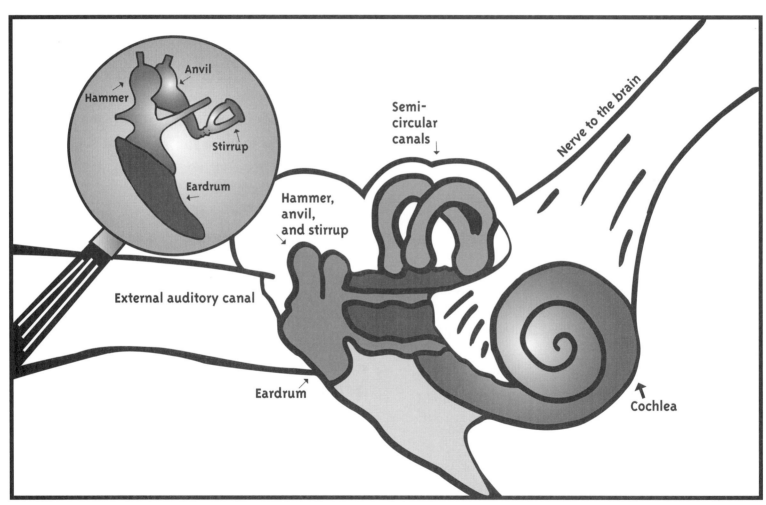

Anvil

Hammer

Stirrup

Eardrum

Semi-circular canals

Nerve to the brain

Hammer, anvil, and stirrup

External auditory canal

Eardrum

Cochlea

Sense-Abilities, ©1998. Published by Chicago Review Press, Inc., 800-888-4741.

American Sign Language

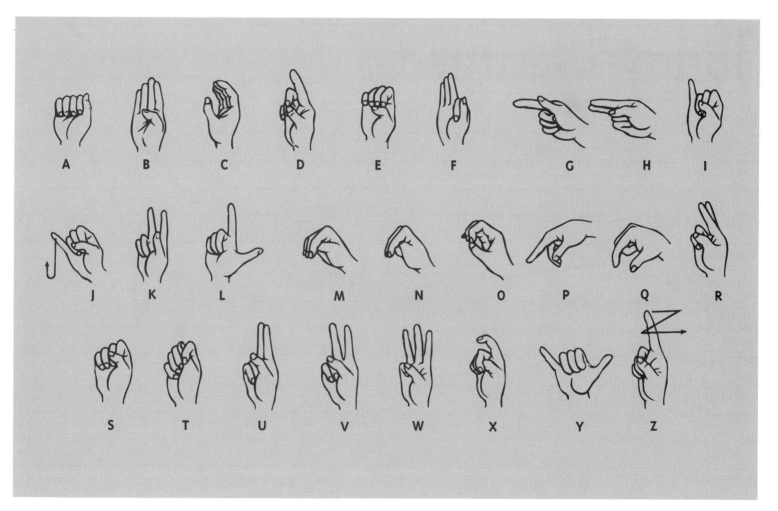

My Sense of Hearing Journal

Today I learned

1 Bending the Ruler—Vivid Vibrations

Did you know?
Every object makes its own vibrations.

You will need
Metal ruler

Encyclopedia
volume or big dictionary

Table or desk

What do you think?
If I push down on a metal
ruler held by a book, it (will) or
(won't) make a sound.

Now you are ready to
1. Place the ruler halfway over the edge of a desk or table. Place the encyclopedia on the section of the ruler lying on the desk.
2. Carefully holding the book down, bend the ruler and let it go.
3. Did the ruler move? How did it move? Did you see the vibrations? Did you hear the vibrations?

Brain exercise
When I pushed the ruler down and let go, . . .

Activity Goal	Sensory Note	Key to Success	Hint
To see and hear vibrations.	Vibrations are caused by movement.	Make sure the ruler is metal, flexible, and positioned safely so it won't hurt the children.	Children need to be careful not to push too hard on the ruler. The ruler can be placed with more or less of it on the table for different sound and vibration effects.

2 Color Ripples—Making Waves

Did you know?

Every sound is made up of vibrations. Vibrations are waves that go through the air. Vibrations cause the molecules in the air to start vibrating. The vibrations move outward in all directions like the ripples created by squeezing a drop of food coloring into water.

You will need

Large bowl of water

Squeezable bottle of dark food coloring

What do you think?

If a drop of food coloring is dropped into the bowl of water, I (will) or (won't) be able to see waves around the drop.

Now you are ready to

1. Observe the water. What does it look like?
2. Drop 1 drop of food coloring into the center of the water.
3. What do you see? Does the water ripple around the drop? Why do you think it is rippling?

Brain exercise

When I saw the food coloring rippling through the water, I thought . . .

Activity Goal	Sensory Note	Key to Success	Hint
To see the rippling effect caused by vibrations.	Vibrations move outward in all directions. They look very similar to the ripples caused by the drop of food coloring.	Only use 1 drop. The darker the color, the better the effect. Adult supervision is needed.	To reinforce this concept, talk about the effect of throwing a stone into a lake.

3 Jumping Peas? Beat the Drum

Did you know?
Vibrations make things move.

You will need
Small coffee can with plastic lid

Large metal spoon

1 teaspoon uncooked split peas (or rice) in a sandwich bag

Partner

What do you think?
If I tap on the coffee-can drum with a spoon, the split peas on top (will) or (won't) jump.

Now you are ready to
1. Make sure the plastic lid is securely placed on the coffee can. It will now become a drum.
2. Hold the drum upright with one arm.
3. Ask your partner to take the split peas out of the sandwich bag and sprinkle them on top of the drum's plastic lid.
3. Using the large metal spoon, have your partner hit the side of the drum.
4. What happened to the peas? Did they move?
5. What caused them to move?
6. Trade places with your partner and try hitting the drum yourself this time.

Brain exercise
When I hit the drum, the peas . . .

Activity Goal	Sensory Note	Key to Success	Hint
To observe peas responding to vibrations.	Vibrations from one object are transferred to another.	Tap on the drum firmly enough to see movement but not so hard that you knock the peas off the lid.	You can also make a drum out of a round oatmeal container with a plastic-wrap top held on by a rubber band.

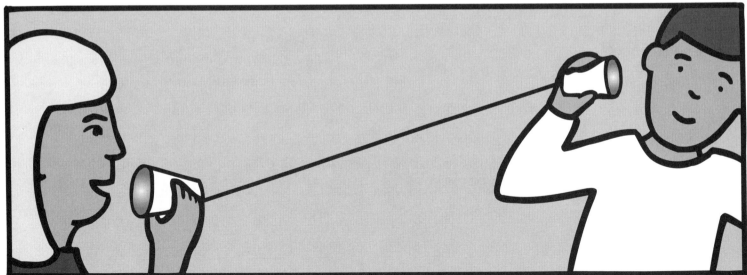

4 Funny Phone Listening Line

Did you know?

Vibrations can travel through string to reach your ears.

For each Funny Phone, you will need

1 5-foot-long piece of string

Plastic needle with large eye (to share)

2 small paper cups

Partner

What do you think?

If I make a listening line using 2 paper cups and a piece of string, I (will) or (won't) be able to use it to talk with my partner.

Now you are ready to

1. Thread the string through the needle.
2. Using the needle, carefully punch a small hole in one of the small paper cups.
3. Pull the string through the hole and tie a large knot.
4. Repeat steps 1 to 3 with the second paper cup.
5. Making sure the string is straight and tight, talk into the cup while your partner holds the other cup up to his/her ear. Could your partner hear you? How do you think this Funny Phone works?

Brain exercise

When I talked into the cup, . . .

Activity Goal	Sensory Note	Key to Success	Hint
To create a fun phone.	Metal cans conduct sound better than paper cups. For safety reasons, we used paper cups.	In order for the Funny Phone to work, the string has to be taut.	This phone is a big hit. Try to make a set for each child.

5 Funneling Tones—Terrific Tubes

Did you know?
Cupping your hand around your ear helps to funnel sound into your ear.

You will need
Empty toilet-paper roll

Empty paper-towel roll

What do you think?
If I listen through an empty toilet-paper roll, I (will) or (won't) be able to hear better.

Now you are ready to
1. Put a toilet-paper roll up to your ear.
2. Listen to the sounds around you.
3. Put the roll down. How are the sounds different from when you were using the roll?
4. Try the same thing with an empty paper-towel roll.
5. Does the sound change?

Brain exercise
The toilet paper roll made my ears . . .

Activity Goal	Sensory Note	Key to Success	Hint
To identify the effect of funneling sound to your ears.	Your ears are shaped to funnel sound waves into your ear canals.	Ask the children to use inside voices.	Decorating the rolls with stickers and markers will make the activity more fun.

6 Sensational Slinking Sounds

Did you know?
Sounds are transmitted through metal very easily.

You will need
Metal Slinky

1 3-foot-long piece of string

What do you think?
If I listen to the string attached to a metal Slinky, I (will) or (won't) be able to hear it vibrate.

Now you are ready to
1. Tie one end of the piece of string to one of the ends of a metal Slinky.
2. Gently twist the other end of the string once around your finger.
3. Place your finger on the outside of your ear.
4. Drop the Slinky onto a hard surface. Listen to the sound it makes.
5. Try moving the Slinky in different directions as you are listening. Do you like the sounds? How are the sounds different from each other?
6. How does the Slinky look? When you drop it can you see a wavelike motion?

Brain exercise
When I dropped the Slinky, my ears . . .

Activity Goal	Sensory Note	Key to Success	Hint
To hear the unique sound vibrations made by a metal Slinky.	Metal Slinkys and metal spoons are great sound conductors.	Make sure no sharp edges are present.	Dropping the Slinky against a desk or uncarpeted floor will give the activity the greatest impact.

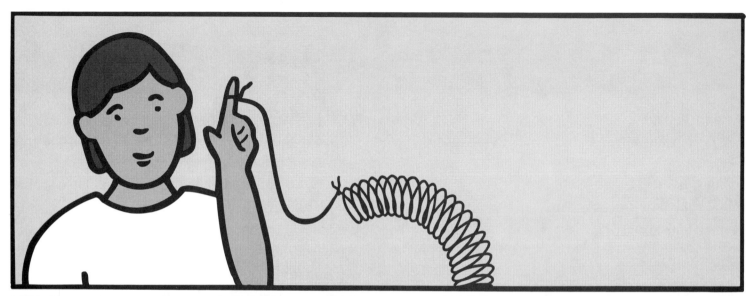

7 Plunging Pebbles—Underwater Sound

Did you know?
Sound is carried four times faster through water than air.

You will need
Large-mouthed glass jar half full of water

4 small pebbles

What do you think?
If I drop pebbles into a jar filled with water, I (will) or (won't) be able to hear the sound.

Now you are ready to
1. Place the jar on a table or counter top.
2. As you place your ear up next to the jar, carefully drop a pebble into the water.
3. Could you hear the pebble drop? Did it sound loud or soft?
4. Carefully drop a similar-sized pebble on the table top. Could you hear the pebble drop? Did it sound louder or softer than when you dropped one into the water?
5. Repeat steps 2 through 4. Did all of the pebbles sound the same?

Brain exercise
When I dropped the pebble into the water, I heard . . .

Activity Goal	Sensory Note	Key to Success	Hint
To listen to sounds through water.	We are able to hear sounds through the air and water.	Make sure the jar is small enough so that it is manageable and large enough so that the child's ear fits next to it.	Adult supervision is necessary.

8 Shake It, Match It

Did you know?
Everything makes its own special sound.

You will need
2 tablespoons each of rice, unpopped popcorn, and chocolate chips

20 metal paper clips

Tablespoon

8 medium-size plastic Easter eggs (or film canisters)

1 empty egg carton for matching and storage

What do you think?
If I shake the plastic eggs filled with rice, I (will) or (won't) be able to match the sounds.

Now you are ready to
1. Place 1 tablespoon of rice inside each of 2 plastic eggs and close them up.
2. Place 10 metal paper clips inside each of 2 plastic eggs and close them up.
3. Repeat step 1 with the rest of your sound samples.
4. As you shake one of the eggs, listen carefully to its special sound.
5. Place the egg inside the egg carton on the lefthand side.
6. Shake another egg. Does it match the first egg's sound? If it does, place it next to the egg it matches.
7. Repeat steps 4 through 6 until you feel that you have matched all of the eggs.
8. Carefully open the eggs to see if they have the same things inside.

Brain exercise
When I shook the matching eggs, my ears told me . . .

Activity Goal	Sensory Note	Key to Success	Hint
To match sounds to themselves.	We can hear sounds and remember them.	All eggs or canisters need to be the same size and shape.	Slightly larger plastic eggs work very well. Children love using them as shaker instruments. Just glue the eggs together and they'll become musical shakers. The eggs can be found all year long at large department stores.

9 Terrific Tunes—Musical Glasses

Did you know?

You can make music with ordinary drinking glasses.

You will need

4 clear drinking glasses the same size and shape

Water

Measuring cups ($^1/_4$, $^1/_2$, $^3/_4$, 1 cup)

Large metal spoon

Food color set (4 squeezable vials)

Record a Tune sheet on page 152, copied onto card stock

What do you think?

If I tap glasses with different amounts of water in them with a metal spoon, they (will) or (won't) all sound the same.

Now you are ready to

1. Pour $^1/_4$ cup of water into one glass, $^1/_2$ cup of water into another, $^3/_4$ cup of water onto another, and 1 cup of water into the last glass. Place 1 drop of food coloring into each glass. Each glass should have a different color.

2. Line up the glasses from the lowest water level to the highest water level.

3. Gently tap each glass with the spoon. Is there any difference in the sounds made by each of the 4 glasses?

4. Make your own music by tapping out a tune on the glasses. Using a copy of the Record a Tune sheet on page 152, record your tune by coloring the right amount of water in each glass. Now you can play your tune whenever you like.

Brain exercise

When I listened to the glasses filled with water, my ears heard . . .

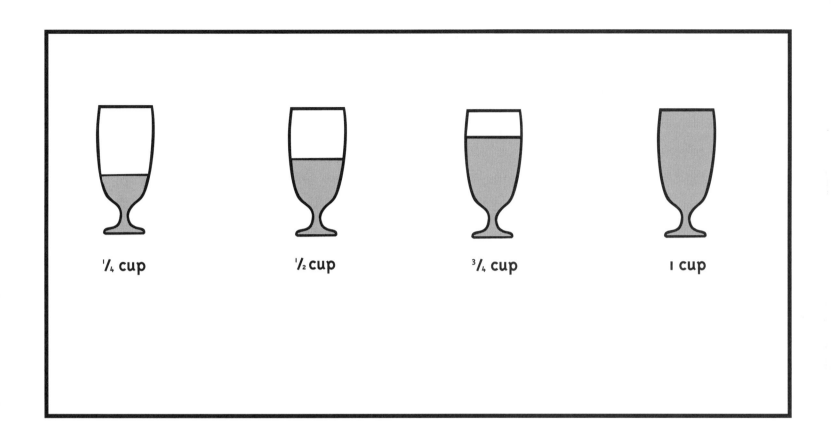

¼ cup ½ cup ¾ cup 1 cup

Record a Tune

Found That Sound? Sound Detectives I

Did you know?

You can locate a sound without using any other sense.

You will need

Partner

Egg timer with a loud ring

What do you think?

If I hear an egg timer, I (will) or (won't) know its location.

Now you are ready to

1. Ask your partner to hide the egg timer (set to go off in 4 minutes) while you close your eyes. Listen for the timer and point to the direction where you think it has been hidden.

2. Get back to whatever you were doing before the egg timer was hidden.

3. When the egg timer rings, see if you were right in your prediction of its hiding spot.

Brain exercise

When I listened for the egg timer, my ears told me . . .

Activity Goal	Sensory Note	Key to Success	Hint
To locate a sound coming from a hidden place in the room.	We use both ears to locate a sound.	If you are working with a large group, the timer needs to be hidden before the children come into the room.	In some cases, children will search for the timer with their eyes. A gentle reminder that we are only using ears helps them focus on hearing.

Did you know?

Musical instruments can be made out of many different items found in your home or school.

You will need

Rubber bands (different sizes and thicknesses)

Boxes (all shapes)

Paper cups (all sizes)

Cans (all sizes)

Pans (different sizes)

What do you think?

If I put a rubber band around a box, it (will) or (won't) make a sound when I pluck it.

Now you are ready to

1. Place a rubber band around a box, paper cup, can, and pan.
2. Pluck the rubber band on each item.
3. Does each rubber band sound the same when plucked?
4. Can you tell what makes the rubber bands sound different?
5. Play with the rubber bands and objects to make sounds you like to hear.

Brain exercise

When I put a rubber band on a pie pan, the sound was . . .

Activity Goal	Sensory Note	Key to Success	Hint
To create musical instruments out of household odds and ends.	Your home and/or school is full of potential instruments.	Allow plenty of time for exploration.	Pie pans are fun to use as instruments, as well as cake pans and odd-shaped boxes.

12 Musical Strings—Pick and Pluck

Did you know?

The thickness of a string or rubber band affects its sound (pitch).

You will need

Long, slender rubber band

Empty coffee can with no top

Fishing line

String

Short, thick rubber band

Unwaxed dental floss (optional)

What do you think?

If I pluck a rubber band, it (will) or (won't) make a different sound than when I pluck a fishing line.

Now you are ready to

1. Place the long, slender rubber band around the length of the coffee can.
2. Place the fishing line and the string across the opening of the can going in the same direction as the rubber band.
3. Take the short, thick rubber band and place it just below the opening around the outside of the can.
4. Pull the fishing line and string until they are tightly secured under the short, thick rubber band.
5. Pluck the fishing line. How does it sound? Pluck the rubber band. How does it sound? Does it sound different than the fishing line? Pluck the string. How does it sound? Is its sound different than that of the fishing line and rubber band?

Brain exercise

When I plucked the fishing line, I heard . . .

Activity Goal	Sensory Note	Key to Success	Hint
To explore the sounds created by different types of materials.	A thick rubber band will have a lower sound than a thin fishing line.	A rubber band that fits snugly around the outside of the can is essential to success.	Try as many types of lines and bands as possible. Each will have its own unique properties and sound.

13 Make a Mini-Megaphone

Did you know?
Sound is magnified by the shape of a megaphone.

You will need
Megaphone form page 158, copied onto
card stock

Stickers

Markers

Scissors

Scotch tape

What do you think?
If I talk into my mini-megaphone, it (will) or (won't)
make a louder sound than if I talk without it.

Now you are ready to
1. Decorate the megaphone with stickers and markers.
2. Cut out the megaphone.
3. Pull the edges of the mini-megaphone together and tape them on the inside and outside.
4. Use your mini-megaphone to talk to your friends.

Brain exercise
When I talked into the megaphone, it . . .

Activity Goal	Sensory Note	Key to Success	Hint
To explore the effect that a mini-megaphone has on sound production.	The mini-megaphone will not magnify sound as much as a full-sized megaphone.	Use card stock instead of paper.	If the children enjoy the mini-megaphone, try making a large megaphone out of card stock for an even greater effect.

Mini-Megaphone

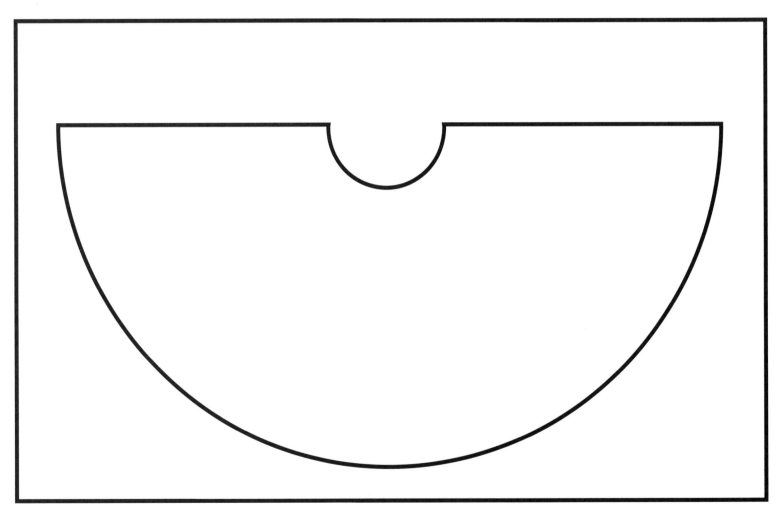

14 Nature and Me—Bird Songs and Sounds

Did you know?
Birds have many different songs and sounds.

You will need
Bird feeder

Mixed birdseed

Cracked sunflower seeds

Black sunflower seeds

Bird identification guide for your area

What do you think?
If I make a kissing sound toward a bird, it (will) or (won't) sing back to me.

Now you are ready to
1. Put up a bird feeder in your yard or visit a yard that has a feeder in it.
2. Check out a bird identification guide for the birds in your area (find a Peterson guide or Audubon guide at your local library or bookstore).
3. Fill the bird feeder with the food recommended in the guidebook. Try to identify the birds you are seeing by their pictures and bird calls.
4. Once the birds start visiting the feeder, stand near the feeder and make soft kissing sounds toward the birds. How do the birds respond? If you are really patient, they will start making sounds back. Listen to their songs and sounds. They are the wonderful sounds of nature.

Brain exercise
When I made a soft kissing sound, the birds . . .

Activity Goal

To expose children to the sounds of nature.

Sensory Note

In the spring, the bird songs are especially beautiful as birds sing their mating calls.

Key to Success

Make sure children don't scare off the birds. They need to walk slowly and quietly.

Hint

Some people use peanut butter to attract the birds. However, peanut butter also attracts mice and rats. Be sure to place the feeder in a spot where other animals won't disturb it.

15 What If? No Sound!

Did you know?
People who can't hear use their other senses to help them make sense of the world.

You will need
Child-size earplugs

Egg timer

American Sign Language Sheet, page 137

What do you think?
If I can't hear, I (will) or (won't) use my other senses to help me.

Now you are ready to
1. Set the timer for 15 minutes.
2. With an adult's help, place the earplugs in your ears. You may still be able to hear a little but not enough to be able to tell what it is that you are hearing.
3. What was it like to be unable to hear? How did you feel when others were talking and you didn't understand what they were saying? Was it harder to tell what was going on around you? What other senses did you use to help you? What dangers might there be if you couldn't hear?
4. Look at page 137. This is American Sign Language. Would you like to learn how to sign so that you could talk with a person who can't hear?

Brain exercise
When I couldn't hear, I felt . . .

Activity Goal	Sensory Note	Key to Success	Hint
To temporarily explore what life might be like without the sense of hearing.	People who are hard of hearing or deaf use sign language to communicate.	Make sure the earplugs fit well and aren't uncomfortable.	This activity may be frustrating for the children. Use this opportunity to further illustrate what life is like for children who can't hear.

16 Walk About and Listen

Did you know?
Sounds are everywhere.

You will need
To be outdoors
Blindfold

What do you think?
If I go outside, I (will) or (won't) be able to hear many wonderful sounds of nature.

Now you are ready to
1. Walk outside and listen. What do you hear?
2. Sit in one spot. Put on the blindfold. Do the sounds change? Do you recognize the sounds? Listen for animal sounds, wind chimes, people sounds, machine sounds, insect sounds, and more.
3. Take off the blindfold. Draw pictures or write about the sounds you heard.

Brain exercise
When I walked outside, I heard . . .

Activity Goal	Sensory Note	Key to Success	Hint
To explore the sounds in your environment.	Sometimes we forget to listen to all the sounds around us.	Adult supervision is necessary.	Wearing a blindfold helps children to focus on the sense of hearing. If you are working with a large group, ask the children to shut their eyes instead of wearing blindfolds.

Acknowledgments

Acknowledgments

Thanks to:

Maureen O'Brien for her thorough review, field-testing, suggestions, and insights.

Professor Bill Muse for his helpful suggestions, review, and inspiration.

Eileen Gibbons for her text review and insightful comments.

Nancy Stewart for her help with the sense of hearing.

Evelyn Sansky for her constant support and inspiration.

Louis Palmer for his recommendations on *Nature and Me —Bird Songs and Sounds*.

Nick and Gid Palmer for their patience and sense of humor.

Nancy Ferrill for her review and helpful comments.

The concierge-level staff at the Empress Hotel in Victoria, Canada, for their support.

Thanks to the following for their flexibility, suggestions, and opening up their classrooms to countless hours of activity testing. This book could not have been written without their support and the contributions of their eager students.

Mrs. Buchan, a preschool teacher at Rainbow Montessori, Redmond, Washington

Mrs. Strain, a kindergarten teacher at East Ridge Elementary School, Woodinville, Washington

Mrs. Brown, a kindergarten teacher at Wilder Elementary School, Woodinville, Washington

Mrs. Richardson, a first-grade teacher at Christa McAuliffe Elementary School, Redmond, Washington

Mrs. Gustin, a first-grade teacher at Horace Mann Elementary School, Redmond, Washington

Thanks to the following for allowing me the opportunity to go through the writing process with their delightful students as content editors. Their students helped with reviewing, testing, and problem-solving issues in the text. Their practical suggestions and efforts contributed significantly to the writing of *Sense-Abilities*.

Ms. Marshall, a fourth-grade teacher at Christa McAuliffe Elementary School, Redmond, Washington

Mr. Pearson, a seventh-grade teacher at Evergreen Junior High School, Redmond, Washington

Mrs. Hanson, an eighth-grade teacher at Redmond Junior High School, Redmond, Washington

Student Contributors

Mrs. Buchan's preschool class

Brianna Bailey
Spencer Bakke
Steven Basque
Max Bennett
Zachary Carnara
Aeron Cardwell
Jacky Chan
Babak Dabagh
Rachel Donnelly
Anna Dye
Spencer Felt
Allison Garcia
Carissa Hargin
Alexandra Hill
Maddie Kinzer
Bronwyn Lamphere
Alex Peterson
Thomas Randall
Ava Runge
Isabel Runge
Chris Schaefer
Jenny Schaefer
Jason Turner

Mrs. Strain's kindergarten class

Kristin Ardourel
Danielle Brenner
Dillon Churchill
Briana Colombo
Andrew Cook
Terri Ellison
Jonathon Forde
Kelly Grindley
Julia Johns
Jesse King
McKenzie Luth
Maya Marder
Colleen McDevitt
Chase Norris
Amy Ransons
Eric Roe
Joseph Scherer
Andrew Schoen
Kevin Shaw
Cortney Simmons
Joseph Sturgeon
Brianna Vail

Mrs. Brown's kindergarten class

Paige Caffey
Sean Callahan
Conor Crowley
Allison D'Angelis
Leah Frank
John Harrison
Cameron Hodges
Parker Imeson
Joe Junor
Jacob Klein
Lauren Minuk
Jared Morris
Devin Nakahara
Kerry Nelson
Kyle Notturno
Rebecca Owen
Ashley Perrin
Colin Porter
Angel Reyers
Christian Rivera
Monica Taylor
Travis Tobin

Mrs. Richardson's first-grade class

Andy Bartholomew
Chris Berg
Kristina Brown
Christian Casolary
Derek Chaney
Alan Chi
Ashley Cleary
Nycole Copping
Asher Dickson
David Evans
Kaitlin Fithian
Megan Kamitsuka
Jenna Kuczynski
Colleen Lorentson
Michael Martel
Brianna Martensen
Caitlin McLuskie
Aasha Morrill
Daniel Neighbors
Benjamin Paholke
Alexander Sanoja
Jake Tyson
David Uno
Peter Vanhoomissen
Kah Xiong

Mrs. Gustin's first-grade class

Julia Ashley
Julia Becerra
Amber Betz
Matthew Carey
John Diiorio
Nicholas Eakle
Serena Eiken
Sarah Flores
Monika Grinbergs
Erika Hendron
Taylor Johnson
Alexine Langdon
Ameen Mainayar
Dylan McBride
Paige Mullins
Steven Munsell
Clara Ng
Denis Ohlstrom
Arianna Pierce
Aidan Pilgrim
Stefany Prescott
Paul Ramtree
Brandon Robinson
Keith Stewart
Jonathon Wooley

Student Contributors

Ms.Marshall's fourth-grade class
Paige Caffey
Grant Beyer
Natalie Bohner
David Breinig
Carolyn Carr
Katy Chapin
Katelyn Davis
Ryan Davis
Cash Elston
Alyson Evans
Chris Howe
Daryl Hutson
Derek Johnson
Kelsey Keizur
Meagan Link
John Meyer
Elaina Methot
Aaron Mortenson
Ryan Newman
James Riley
Jennifer Schroder
Jacob Smith
Emily Steyer
Daniel Williams

Mr. Pearson's seventh-grade class
Beau Amick
Elias Asberry
Benjamin Beckwith
Kevin Couts
Kacie DuBois
Kevin Farrow
Miles Flint
Lauren Guezuraga
Sara Hammersberg
Chris Holland
Adam Kaley
Joshua Kaushansky
Tom Larkin
Craig Liljegren
Neill Marshall
Matthew Peteshel
Robert Powell
Thomas Rismoen
John Rudolph
Shawn Schoonover
Beau Shirdavani
Kellie Sorlien
Jeremy Thompson
Michelle Trager
Kathryn Whelchel
Lisa Wyatt

Mrs. Hanson's eighth-grade class
Ben Backes
James Bayley
Jessica Boegel
Catlyn Caldart
Ro-el Cordero
Tamra Dickson
Kelly Fahl
Jocelyn Farenbaugh
Francesco Forin
Matt Hill
Cathy Karlak
Rosie MacDonald-Schmidt
Zack Marley
Kelsey Mays
Ashley Mertens
Melissa Murray
Stephen Oliver
Nick Palmer
Andrea Palmiter
Erin Ramsey
Jane Rowell
Alex Schmidt
Julie Schulman
Stephen Simon
Quynh-Nhu Tran
Brian Yeh

Mrs. O'Brien's homeschool class
Kaleigh O'Brien
Kevin O'Brien
Kieran O'Brien